Toobeez Teambuilding Activity Workbook

Fostering Connections and Teamwork Through Fun!

Author
Tom Heck

Adapted from the award-winning book
The Official Toobeez Team Building Games and Activity Guide

Editor
Victoria Anderson

Reviewed by
Timothy G. Arem, Candice Donnelly-Knox, Joseph A. Donahue, B. Michael McCarver, Albert J. Reyes & Victoria Anderson

Cover designed by Mark Broomell of mbDesignworks
Project Connect website and systems designed by
Bruce Ross of www.DigitalTek.com

www.project-connect.net   www.TeachMeTeamwork.com

Award-Winning!

Tested in 2004 by multiple teachers with families, the Toobeez Interactive Family Edition has won a Teacher's Choice Award for 2005. The Interactive Family Edition is what you get when you combine a set of Toobeez with Tom Heck's book, *The Official Toobeez Team Building Games and Activity Guide*, and Multimedia Training CD.

All Project Connect Joint Venture participants are members of the following organizations

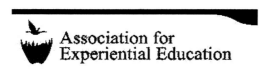

About the Author

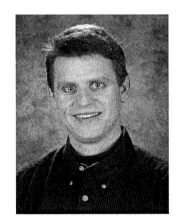

My first introduction to Toobeez was in the spring of 2004 when Joe Donahue, the inventor of Toobeez, called me to see if I would write a teambuilding activity guide for his product. He sent me a box of Toobeez, and I was immediately hooked. I have been working in the field of experiential education for most of my adult life, and through this workbook, I hope to share many of the insights I have gained about working with groups.

Tom Heck

After earning a degree in education from Virginia Tech, I worked for two and half years as a Juvenile Corrections Officer in a wilderness therapeutic program. It was there that I began to understand the amazing world of experiential education.

I went on to teach Technology Education in a public high school in the suburbs of Washington D.C. I discovered as a high school teacher that most of my students were extremely deficient in team and leadership skills. It was then that I dedicated my life to teaching these valuable skills.

I moved on to work for the YMCA where I channeled my energy into teaching team and leadership skills to students in elementary, middle and high schools. Most of my programs were school-based, and in five years, I had shared team and leadership development strategies with over 10,000 students!

In 1996, I created a training and development company to teach team and leadership skills on a national and international level. I also began inventing teambuilding games and now have over 20 of them which are sold worldwide. In 2002, I developed and launched a web-based training solution called **www.TeachMeTeamwork.com**. Through this website, I have taught over 15,000 people in 71 countries how to lead teambuilding games, and I have supported educators, trainers and organizations in developing and delivering teambuilding training curriculum and events.

Come to my website and signup for a FREE teambuilding games e-newsletter. When you signup, I will send you a FREE teambuilding games book.

Project Connect thanks the following people for reviewing this guide.

Tom Heck

Team and Leadership Coach and author of *The Official Toobeez Teambuilding Games and Activity Guide* and Multimedia Training CD. Through my new easy-to-use website, I train all types of educators in over 70 countries how to lead fun and engaging teambuilding games. Free teambuilding games e-book and newsletter are available.

 teachmeteamwork.com

Contact:
World Headquarters
P.O. Box 1831
Asheville, NC 28802
828-665-0303
www.TeachMeTeamwork.com

Joseph A. Donahue

Project Connect Joint Venture Manager and inventor of the Toobeez™ giant construction building system. It is our mission to develop innovative and thought-provoking educational products for kids and adults. Please visit us for more information at www.project-connect.net.

Contact:
Connectable Color Tubes, LLC
c/o Educational Products Division
1204 Thomas Road
Wayne, PA 19087
877-TOOBEEZ
877-866-2339

Victoria Anderson, M.Ed.

Author of the *Toobeez Language Arts Activity Workbook* and Independent Writing Consultant. Anderson Editorial Services is a company dedicated to providing writing services for creative, informational and educational writing. Whether developing, editing, formatting or proofreading, Anderson Editorial is committed to producing the highest quality of writing.

Contact:
Anderson Editorial Services
Cherry Hill, NJ
732-616-7421
www.andersoneditorialservices.com

4

Lingua Medica LLC

B. Michael McCarver, JD and Albert J. Reyes, MA are the principals of Lingua Medica LLC, a partnership of educational writers, researchers and analysts specializing in science, mathematics and medical education, and co-authors of the *Toobeez Math Activity Workbook*. Their goal is to create successful educational materials by fusing quality writing with effective presentation formats.

Contact:
Lingua Medica LLC
229 Grant Avenue
Jersey City, NJ 07305
201-792-9419
www.linguamedica.net

Candice Donnelly-Knox, OTR/L

Author of the *Toobeez Occupational Therapy Activity Workbook*. As an occupational therapist serving the pediatric population in the educational setting, I have experience working with students with a variety of special needs. It is a challenge and a joy to collaborate with families, teachers and the team to generate positive and creative learning experiences for children of all abilities! I am thrilled to be dedicated to such an amazing group of children!

Contact:
Candice Donnelly-Knox, OTR/L
Pottstown, PA 19464
Brainwaves4kids@aol.com
Fax: 610-326-6996

Timothy G. Arem, M.Ed.

Health and fitness family consultant and author of the *Toobeez Physical Education Activity Workbook*. Empowering 100,000 families per year with the message of being active and making healthy choices from childhood to adulthood.

Contact:
T-Bone Productions International
1207 River Ridge Drive
Asheville, NC 28803
828-298-4789
www.TboneRun.com

Vicky Pitner, CTRS

Author of the *Toobeez Senior Therapy Activity Workbook*. Recreation Services provides therapeutic recreation consulting, workshops, staff and respite training, program development and more!

Contact:
Vicky Pitner, CTRS
Recreational Services, Inc.
Franklin, TN
615-585-1188
www.recreationservices.net

Project Connect
Training Opportunities

Do you want to:

- Become a more effective educator, teacher or trainer?
- Learn to creatively increase student involvement?
- Develop strategies for creating a dynamic learning environment?
- Experience what it is like to work as a high-performing team?
- Improve your students' ability to understand and retain information?
- Gain greater control of the learning environment?
- Teach AND have fun?
- Learn to draw out the genius within your group?

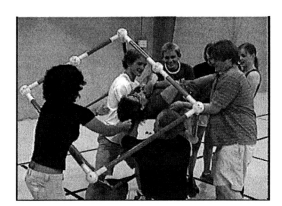

If you answered yes to any of the above questions, then the Project Connect training workshops are for you! We offer two types of workshops:

1. Train-the-Trainer Workshop
2. TEAM Workshop

Train-the-Trainer Workshop

Project Connect Train-the-Trainer workshops are for educators of all types who are looking for new ways to teach team and leadership skills in a fun and engaging environment. In a Train-the-Trainer workshop, you can expect to learn ways to incorporate teambuilding activities into your existing curriculum.

Our trainers have worked in the field of team and leadership development training for over a decade. We have worked with nearly every kind of educational situation you can imagine - from fourth grade students to groups of high-end account representatives. All of the groups were unique, and yet they all had one thing in common. They wanted to come together and work better as a team. When we work with your group, we will bring this level of experience with us and share our knowledge freely and energetically.

The Train-the-Trainer workshop is for you if:
- You are an educator teaching team and leadership skills
- You like learning in a fast-paced and hands-on environment

What to expect
In the Train-the-Trainer workshop, you will learn how to lead activities that develop team and leadership skills. This workshop is fun, empowering and educational. It is also experiential, meaning you will learn by doing.

You will learn activities that promote trust and creative problem solving, as well as encourage purposeful communication. You will experience physical activities, as well as activities which demand high cerebral skills. You will learn how to design everything from a five-minute icebreaker to a full two-day adventure. Depending on the length of the program you choose, you can even learn how to integrate the activities into an existing curriculum.

You will learn how to deliver important debriefing and processing skills by asking thought-provoking questions in order to draw out the genius of a group. When a debriefing session is delivered properly, groups learn to own the information they generate from the teambuilding activities, providing them with a sense of empowerment, connectedness and success!

7

We can teach you HOW and WHY groups do the things they do. In our longer workshops, we cover topics such as:

- Group Theory
- The Seven Characteristics of High-Performing Teams
- How Great Leaders Apply Their Knowledge of the Six Human Needs
- The Four Classes of Human Experience
- The Four Stages of Group Development
- Top Eight Behaviors to Observe in Groups
- Four Leadership Styles and How to Match Them to the Situation
- Beliefs of Great Leaders
- Seven Levels of Influencing
- The I-N-W Model of Coaching as a Leadership Tool

This is the perfect workshop for you if you are a:

- Classroom teacher
- School counselor
- Camp counselor
- Human Resources director
- Trainer or workshop presenter
- Therapeutic Recreation Specialist
- Public speaker

Workshop length runs from a 90-minute introductory session to a four-day intensive program.

TEAM Workshop

TEAM
Together Everyone Achieves More

Do you have an intact team? Is your team ready to move from good to great?

Over the years, we have worked with thousands of people from all walks of life, including:
- Business teams in various industries (such as investing, communications, insurance and accounting)
- Non-profit organizations (such as YMCA, YWCA and Boys & Girls Clubs)
- Educators (including public and private school teachers, school counselors, college students, college teaching staff and international students)
- Alternative education programs (including corrections officers, after-school programs and enrichment programs)

The TEAM workshop is for your team if you are ready to:
- Move quickly from a "good" team to a "great" team
- Have fun and be challenged in a dynamic learning environment
- Be treated with respect and dignity while leveraging the strengths of your group

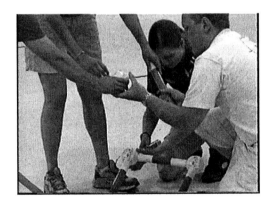

What to expect
In this workshop, you will participate in fun and engaging hands-on learning exercises to help your team address vital issues. This workshop focuses on where you are now as a group and where you are going.

9

Our approach to evolving teams starts by asking what the *individuals* do right now to bring about positive change. We promote taking *personal* responsibility and *immediate* responsible action. This workshop uses the best Toobeez problem-solving activities, and because we work with you ahead of time to determine the needs and desires of your particular group, all the exercises are appropriate for your team.

There are those who believe a one-day workshop is going to be the answer to long-term team success. These are often the same people who believe that working out at the gym once a year makes them healthy and fit. It just does not work that way. The health enthusiast must invest a great deal of time and energy at the gym for months before he is able to reap the rewards of his efforts.

For a team to exhibit the characteristics of a high-impact team, they must practice, practice, practice, and the Toobeez workshops are a great tool to provide the needed practice.

For more information about attending or scheduling teambuilding training workshops, call:

1-877-TOOBEEZ
1-877-866-2339

Table of Contents

www.project-connect.net   www.TeachMeTeamwork.com

Special Thanks

We would like to thank the staff of the YMCA Blue Ridge Assembly for all of their work in front of the camera. All of the people you see in the photos and the Multimedia Training CD video clips are YMCA Blue Ridge Assembly staff. We have known the people associated with this facility for many years, and they are always kind, courteous, knowledgeable and enthusiastic. They have an outstanding facility and an amazing adventure-learning program. You will do well to hold your next event at the YMCA Blue Ridge Assembly. www.blueridgeassembly.org

Introduction

Project Connect is dedicated to providing cutting-edge teambuilding activities and tools for educators. These activities can be used for exciting teambuilding days and can reinforce everyday moments with both youth and adults!

Project Connect offers the following products:

Toobeez

Toobeez are the incredible construction tubes used to build and create the activities for your group! A one-of-a-kind construction system, Toobeez give you the chance to "connect" as a group while engaging everybody in constructive play. Toobeez are a hands-on, easy-to-assemble and safe product that captivates the imagination of anyone who uses them. You can use them indoors or outdoors to hold a powerful teambuilding experience anytime!

Each 57 Piece Toobeez Kit contains: (20) 3.4" spheres, (8) 36" tubes, (8) 24" tubes, (8) 16" tubes, (8) 11" tubes, (1) GIANT Toobeez storage bag, (2) red slide-on curtain panels, & (2) blue slide-on curtain panels. Shipping box is 36" x 12" x 6" and weighs 21 lbs.

Activity Workbooks

The *Toobeez Teambuilding Activity Workbook* includes 25 detailed lesson plans with safety reminders, helpful hints, procedures, debriefing questions and more to build and develop the communication and teambuilding skills of your group. Other available workbooks include Math, Science, Language Arts, Physical Education and Occupational Therapy.

Multimedia Training CD

This CD is based on the award-winning book by Tom Heck entitled *The Official Toobeez Team Building Games Activity Guide.* This CD contains all of the information found in the guide plus video clips, audio interviews and other special bonus features. Purchase your CD today at www.teachmeteamwork.com.

13

A Leadership Note

Who you are as a leader dramatically affects how your students learn from you. Some leaders think that the teambuilding activities will carry an adventure program, however this is a common misconception. The truth is the more developed you are as a person, the more likely your participants will experience positive growth and development both individually and as a team.

There are many types of personal development programs that will advance your skills as a teambuilding coach. Some people believe a one-day workshop is the answer to long-term team success, but it does not work that way. This thought process can be compared to those people who believe that working out at the gym once a year makes them healthy and fit. On the contrary - the health enthusiast must invest a great deal of time and energy at the gym for months before he is able to reap the rewards of his efforts. The same principal goes for exceptional personal development programs. There are no "quick fixes" along this path. Success as a teacher and facilitator through personal development takes time, energy and commitment.

I offer an intensive, year-long coaching program for individuals or groups designed to advance personal and professional development for educators and facilitators of teams. To find out more about this program, view the "coaching" description on my website, www.teachmeteamwork.com.

The Activity as Metaphor
These activities are wonderful, and they can have a positive effect on your group. The key to learning through experiential teambuilding exercises is the combination of activity and discussion. Hopefully, these activities will be utilized to create opportunities for meaningful dialogue, however the activities described here can be done just for fun without going into a discussion about what was learned. Suggestions for starting a conversation are offered in each description.

Individual Choice
Each activity in this program should be led so that participants understand they have a choice as to whether they participate or not. Encourage each person to determine their comfort level with the activity and to join in at the level they choose (full, partial or none) rather than be coerced into participation.

Connections to Education

Toobeez are a unique means of teaching social skills, teamwork and problem solving. For the first time, the Toobeez program has been adapted as a useful teaching tool for utilization in schools and educational forums. The lesson plans developed with Toobeez are designed to challenge students to evaluate concepts from a practical point of view with hands-on learning opportunities.

Teachers can use Toobeez as an innovative tool to implement the current educational practices discussed below. In addition, use of Toobeez in the classroom can play an important role in establishing connections between students, peers and teachers!

Brain-based Research

The Toobeez program activities support brain-based research by engaging learners and providing enjoyable hands-on experiences. The essence of brain research suggests that all learners have emotions, desires and needs. Researchers have found that relaxed, yet active, lessons that completely immerse the participants provide the most authentic learning experiences. This type of environment has been shown to increase retention, enjoyment and positive feelings about learning. The Toobeez program provides activities that challenge each participant at his or her individual level while engrossing them in a fun-filled learning environment.

Multiple Intelligence Theory

Developed in 1983 by Dr. Howard Gardner, the Multiple Intelligence Theory states there are multiple learning styles that maximize the learning potential in children and adults. The theory takes into account the various strengths in individuals, such as linguistic, logical, spatial and kinesthetic skills. It suggests that different people learn in different ways. The Toobeez program provides a unique way to broaden the learning experience beyond traditional methods. By allowing instructors to offer lessons which address different learning styles, learning increases across the classroom.

Differentiated Instruction

In addition to building on the varying strengths of individuals, the Toobeez program allows instructors to appropriately adapt lessons to the various ability levels in a classroom. Activities can be enhanced for a greater challenge or they can be modified

15

for a simpler activity. Also, individuals are encouraged to participate at their own level of comfort so all participants experience success.

Problem Solving

Lesson plans and activities in the Toobeez program require critical thinking and problem solving skills. Participants are required to work together to brainstorm, select and execute solutions to each activity challenge.

Character Education Themes

Helping young people develop good character is a goal of many educational settings nationwide. The Toobeez program offers activities that can supplement or launch a character education curriculum. The character themes listed below have been aligned with the activities in this guide, and the first page of each activity associates a character education trait with the activity.

- Trust	- Teamwork/Cooperation	- Uniqueness
- Respecting Others	- Citizenship	- Caring
- Communication	- Responsibility	- Perseverance

Teambuilding & Connections with Others

Research has shown that a sense of "connectedness" to parents and peers is the most influential protective factor in a teenager's life. If teenagers lack this connection, their chance of engaging in risky behaviors increases. Through increasing teambuilding skills, the Toobeez program brings peers together while boosting the individual's self-confidence and sense of "connectedness" with others.

Collaborative Hands-On Experience

The Toobeez program centers around a collaborative learning environment. Groups work together to solve each challenge while completing interactive, hands-on activities. Each lesson involves member participation, movement and teamwork for completion of the activity.

16

The Facilitator's Role

The facilitator plays a crucial role in the Toobeez program's activities. After selecting the activity, the facilitator must aid participants in executing the instructions, monitor safety, and observe the group's dynamics. Most important, it is the facilitator's responsibility to convey positive leadership and the potential for success to create the best environment for these teambuilding activities.

Motivational Teambuilding Guide

Once the facilitator determines that an activity is suitable for a particular group, he or she must make judgments about how the group is working. The facilitator is responsible for running the activity; however, he or she should not run the group. Instead, the facilitator should act as a guide for participants and ask probing questions which will help the group to progress in the activity. The facilitator should positively motivate participants so each individual enjoys the best possible teambuilding experience.

Safety Patrol

Several of the activities in this guide require lifting participants. After determining if a group is ready for such an activity, the facilitator must make sure all the participants have learned how to spot. In addition, the facilitator must encourage participants to focus while taking on the responsibility of spotting and lifting. It is the responsibility of the facilitator to ensure the activity is conducted in the safest possible manner.

Observer

While running the activity, the facilitator must allow participants to solve problems on their own. When groups are working, the facilitator should take a step away and observe the group's dynamics so he or she can guide the group appropriately if they encounter problems.

Discussion Coordinator

The facilitator begins the discussion by asking the questions he or she feels are most appropriate for the group. While considering the lessons learned from a challenge, as well as the possible "failures," the facilitator should focus on the group's positive learning experiences while acknowledging both negative and positive issues.

The Element of Risk

Challenge and adventure activities can present elements of physical and emotional risk. While this activity guide serves as an introduction to the use of adventure-based experiential learning, it is only an introduction. Studying the material in this activity guide is not a substitute for professional training. Please refer to pages 6 - 10 for information regarding the training options offered by Project Connect. For additional safety information, as well as product assembly and care, please turn to page 173.

It is not possible to run a perfectly safe program since "safe" infers an absence of risk. Experiential learning is adventuresome because of the presence of risk. It is impossible to remove all risk from adventure-learning activities (the type of activities you will read about in this activity guide) since eliminating all risk removes the trust-building elements of the activities and renders the activities useless.

The information presented in this activity guide is a reference, and the facilitator is ultimately responsible for judging the suitability of an activity and safely supervising the activity.

> ## The facilitator's job is to make safety a <u>priority</u> and to <u>manage</u> the risk.

The publisher of this document assumes no responsibility or liability for the use of the information presented in this guide, including, but not limited to, errors due to misprinting or omission of detail.

Safety Procedures

The following list provides suggested strategies for managing risk in this adventure program:

1. Group members are encouraged to participate at their own level of comfort. Coercion is not part of the program.
2. Programs, companies and schools should develop a safety policy.
3. All participants should sign a "Participant Agreement, Indemnification and Acknowledgment of Risk for Minors" form. This document can be created with the help of a competent attorney.
4. Staff must be trained in risk management, CPR and first aid.
5. A first-aid kit and telephone must be on the premises and easily accessible.
6. Inspect all props prior to and after use.
7. The location must be free of dangers or hazards.
8. Participants should be given a safety briefing before beginning the program.
9. Participants should be led in stretching and warm-up activities at the beginning of a program.
10. When activities call for lifting, participants must be taught proper spotting techniques (see below).
11. Staff must always support and protect the head of a participant who is being lifted or lowered.

The Importance of Spotting

Some of the activities presented in this activity guide require participants to lift each other off the ground. This can be dangerous for both the lifters and the person being lifted. For this reason, the facilitator must convey the importance of proper spotting.

Spotting is the art of protecting a team member's head and upper body from the impact of a fall by creating a cushion to effectively slow their fall. Spotting does not mean you catch a person when they fall.

Effective spotting requires that all participants pay close attention to the activity. If members of the group are not ready to participate in an activity that requires spotting, choose another activity.

19

To be effective spotters, participants must have a high degree of trust. If participants are engaging in horseplay or are using language (or other forms of communication) that takes away from the feeling of trust, please reconsider using any activity that involves spotting.

Spotting is a difficult task to teach because the potential spotter usually does not recognize its importance until they actually have to support a falling body.

The following are pointers for teaching spotting:
1. Explain the concept and meaning of spotting as described above.
2. Practice spotting with participants before they actually need to use the skill in an activity.
3. The facilitator must model spotting.
4. A good spotter shares the responsibility of spotting equally. It is easier and safer to work as a team when spotting.
5. Spotters should stand in a balanced position, holding their hands up in a "ready" position.
6. The spotter's focus must remain on the participant at all times.
7. Spotters must cushion a fall, moving with the direction of force. <u>Do not</u> attempt to catch and hold a falling participant.
8. Teasing and joking about not catching someone is an unsafe attitude that should not be permitted.
9. The activities in this guide which involve lifting require a minimum number of two spotters. Depending on the skill and ability level of your particular group, more spotters may be necessary.
10. Supervise the spotters closely.

How to Use This Workbook

Lesson Introduction Page
The first page of each lesson contains an outline of information for the facilitator. This page includes lesson objectives, links to character themes, the activity challenge and setup procedures.

An **Activity Plan** box on the page includes information regarding group size and time requirements. <u>Mental and physical intensities</u> are rated on a scale of 1 to 3 (with 1 being the least intense and 3 being the most intense). <u>Space requirements</u> are defined as follows:

> **Minimal**: Activity can be conducted in the front of the room
> **Medium**: A few desks or some furniture may need to be moved
> **Lots**: Clear all desks/furniture or relocate to the gym or an outdoor area

Safety Reminders
This section contains specific safety reminders for each activity. Please be sure to read the "Safety" section in the beginning of this guide, and always follow general safety precautions for each activity.

Helpful Hints
This section provides the facilitator with suggestions to help guide the participants and avoid possible obstacles during the activity.

Activity Instructions
This section provides step-by-step instructions for the facilitator to follow.
- **Storyline** - Use the storyline to excite participants about the activity
- **Activity Challenge** - Each activity presents a specific challenge to the participants. Be sure to read this box to the group and clarify their understanding of the challenge

- **Problem-Solving Sequence** – Before beginning the activity, have the participants work through the Problem Solving Sequence. The steps for this sequence are also located in Appendix A for reference. These steps are:
    1. Circle up
    2. Know and understand the challenge and the guidelines
    3. Brainstorm
    4. Make a plan
    5. Do the plan
    6. Evaluate results and adjust as necessary

Activity Variations
This section provides variations for easier or more challenging versions of the activity.

Notes
Space is provided for the facilitator's notes on the activity. Notes can help facilitators reflect on the lesson, as well as record possible future modifications.

Activity Discussion and Processing
This section provides the facilitator with a discussion topic that relates to the activity, as well as support information to use in guiding a group discussion. Questions are provided for the facilitator to help guide the discussion.

ACTIVITY 1

ALL ABOARD

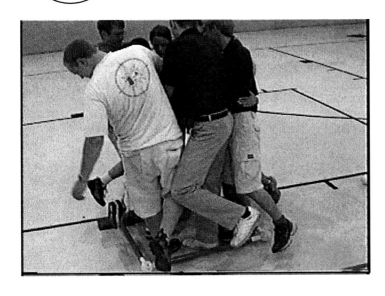

Objectives

- Collaborate with team members to develop strategies to fit inside the Toobeez square
- Utilize teamwork skills to complete the activity
- Participate in a group conversation to process and evaluate the experience

Preparation

Time: 1 minute
Materials: 1 Toobeez set
chart paper (optional)

Setup:
1. Create a large square using four of the longest tubes.

The Challenge

The entire group must fit inside the Toobeez square.

Character Focus

Teamwork

Activity Plan

Group Size: 8 - 20

Time: 15 - 60 minutes

Mental Intensity: 2

Physical Intensity: 3

Space: Medium

23

Safety Reminders!

Appropriate caution is important to conduct these activities in a safe manner. Be sure to review these reminders prior to beginning the activity, and if necessary, share reminders with the group during the activity.

- Closed-toed shoes must be worn. No bare feet or sandals
- Do not allow participants to pile up or climb on anyone's back or shoulders
- Remember to council the group not to fall on top of anyone
- Spot the group, and make sure to prevent head and back injuries
- Do not allow participants to lock elbows
- Do not allow participants to stand on other people's feet

- Four of the largest Toobeez create a square that holds 15 adults who are working well as a team

Activity Instructions

1. Circle up the group, and share the following storyline.

> Your team's ship is sinking. The Coast Guard is on the way, but the waters are shark-infested and only a small portion of your ship remains above the water. Get your team on what is left of the ship and the sharks will stay away. The rescue ship is almost here!

24

2. Read aloud the following Activity Challenge Box to the group.

> **Challenge**: The entire group must fit inside the Toobeez square. Follow the guidelines below:
> - Everyone must be touching the inside of the square
> - The group must remain touching inside the square for a certain length of time (for example, the time it takes to sing one round of "Row, Row, Row Your Boat")
> - During the song, no one can touch the ground outside the square
> - No one may stand on the Toobeez
> - The Toobeez square may not be altered in any way
> - If any guidelines are broken, the group must begin again

3. To begin the activity, have participants first work through the Problem-Solving Sequence (refer to page 152 for the six sequence steps).
4. Be sure to monitor the group for safety as they attempt the activity.
5. If participants get stuck, have the students circle up again. Use questions to help guide the group back on track, but do not provide the participants with answers. Allow them to work together.
6. If your group is still struggling OR if you feel your group would benefit from an additional challenge, present a variation provided on the next page.
7. After the activity, move to the "Activity Discussion and Processing" section of the activity.

> See page 6 for available teambuilding training options!

25

All Aboard

Activity Variations

1. Adding a challenge.
After the group experiences success, create a square that is slightly smaller. Reduce the size of the square with each success.

2. Create an imaginary river.
Have the group use multiple squares as "stepping stones" to cross the river. Do not allow anyone to cross to the other side of the riverbank until there is no one left on the side from where they started.

Activity Notes

Acknowledgments
Karl Rohnke provided a description of this activity in his book, *Silver Bullets,* published in 1984.

www.project-connect.net   www.TeachMeTeamwork.com

All Aboard

Activity Discussion and Processing

Discussion Topic: What is "impossible?"

Oftentimes, the only thing that limits us is our beliefs. When something is viewed as impossible, it is usually because of the limiting beliefs someone holds. An example of this might include beliefs from several centuries ago that the world was flat. Later in the early 1800's, if you told someone that people would be able to communicate with each other around the world instantaneously (that is, by telephone) or that we would fly to the moon and back, you would have encountered much laughter. If a person believes something is possible, they will take different actions than if they believe it is impossible.

Discussion Topic: Failure

As the group solves each challenge, gradually make the useable platform space smaller. The group will get to a point where the challenge is greater than their ability to solve it in the given amount of time. Then, ask the group if their inability to solve the challenge means they are a failure. You will find that some people in the group have rules for themselves that make failure easy to achieve. For example, "In order for me to fail, all I have to know is that I did not complete a given task." Others in the group will have rules that make failure hard to achieve. For example, "In order for me to fail, I must not learn anything. As long as I learn something, I have succeeded."

Questions for Discussion

- What did our group have to believe in order to be successful?
- What are your rules about "failure?" Do they serve you?
- Babe Ruth, the famous baseball home run hitter and hall of famer, also held a record for having the most strike outs in a season. Is Babe Ruth remembered as a failure or a hero? Why?

Motivator

Discuss the following quote with participants.

> "Whether you think that you can, or that you can not, you are usually right."
> - *Henry Ford, Inventor, automotive pioneer and founder of Ford Motor Company*

27

ACTIVITY 2  AMOEBA ELECTRIC FENCE

Objectives
- Collaborate with team members to develop strategies to move the group over the fence
- Communicate and cooperate with team members
- Rely on team members
- Participate in a group conversation to process and evaluate the experience

Preparation
Time: 5 minutes
Materials: 1 Toobeez set
15 - 20 foot piece rope
chart paper (optional)
Setup:
1. Set up the "electric fence" at an appropriate level of challenge for the group. The taller the height, the harder the task. **Note:** The second longest tube makes a good challenge for middle school students.

Character Focus
Trust & Caring

Activity Plan
Group Size: 5 - 20
Time: 15 - 45 minutes
Mental Intensity: 2
Physical Intensity: 3
Space: Medium

The Challenge
The entire group must cross over the "electric fence" without touching the Toobeez and without letting go of the rope.

28

Amoeba Electric Fence

Safety Reminders!

Appropriate caution is important to conduct these activities in a safe manner. Be sure to review these reminders prior to beginning the activity, and if necessary, share reminders with the group during the activity.

- Introduce/review spotting techniques and safety procedures with all participants (refer to the "Safety Procedures" section on page 19)
- Proper spotting is necessary so participants do not hit their head or spine on the ground. It is ideal to have cushions or pads placed under the horizontal bar of the fence to minimize the effects if a fall occurs
- If your group is not physically strong enough, mature enough and/or calm enough, do not attempt this activity
- For more suggestions, refer to the "Activity Discussion and Processing" section

- This challenge requires a lot of trust and is best left for a mature group that is able to consider the safety of others
- Consider presenting this activity in stages, beginning with a low fence height so the group can easily travel over the fence
- The "lifeline" requires the group to stay focused and to keep their "head in the game"

Activity Instructions

1. Circle up the group, and share the following storyline.

> Your team is being held captive by an evil giant. The giant has built an electric fence to keep you from freedom. In addition, the giant has made it impossible (or so he thinks) for you to cross the fence by magically joining your entire team together. Cross the fence and you will be free to live the life of your dreams.

Amoeba Electric Fence

2. Read aloud the following Activity Challenge Box to the group.

Challenge: The entire group must cross over the "electric fence" without touching the Toobeez and without letting go of the rope. Follow the guidelines below:

- The group may not utilize the space directly under the horizontal bar of the fence
- No one may touch the fence or any supporting Toobeez
- Everyone must hold on to the "lifeline" rope
- All members of the team must have at least one hand on the lifeline rope throughout the activity
- No other supplies may be used in this activity
- A team member crossing over the fence must remain in physical contact with at least one other teammate all times
- If any guidelines are broken, the group must begin again

---

3. To begin the activity, have participants first work through the Problem-Solving Sequence (refer to page 152 for the six sequence steps).
4. Ask the participants to name some of their obstacles. Suggest to the group that the electric fence represents these obstacles.
5. Be sure to monitor the group for safety as they attempt the activity.
6. If participants get stuck, have the students circle up again. Use questions to help guide the group back on track, but do not provide the participants with answers. Allow them to work together.
7. If your group is still struggling OR if you feel your group would benefit from an additional challenge, present a variation provided on the next page.
8. After the activity, move to the "Activity Discussion and Processing" section of the activity.

See page 6 for available teambuilding training options!

Activity Variations

1. Provide a shorter lifeline to participants.
Use your best judgment. Pick a length that you know will challenge them further but still be possible.

2. Divide the group into smaller groups.
Have the two groups start on opposite sides of the fence, and provide each group with their own lifeline. The groups should then switch places.

Activity Notes

Acknowledgments
A variation on this activity was first written up in Karl Rohnke's book, *Silver Bullets,* published in 1984.

Amoeba Electric Fence

Activity Discussion and Processing

Discussion Topic: Goals

Prior to the activity starting, ask the group to do the following:

- Identify your dreams and goals, both individually and as a team. Write them down on index cards and place them on a chair on the other side of the fence
- Identify some of the obstacles ("fences") that stand between you and your dreams and goals. Write these on index cards and tape the cards to the Toobeez fence. The fence represents all the obstacles that stand in your way
- Identify your strengths, skills and attributes both individually and collectively. Write them on index cards and place them in a special bucket or container. The group must carry this bucket with them throughout the activity

Questions for Discussion

- Was the obstacle (fence) easier or harder to get over than what you had originally thought?
- Did you use all the strengths, skills and attributes of your team? Describe
- Did you use skills not originally listed? If yes, which ones? When did you use them?
- Are the goals you listed worth the hard effort?
- Would you like to add a new goal or two?

Motivator

Discuss the following with the participants.

"Four Lessons on Life" by Warren Wiersbe:

1. Never take down a fence until you know why it was put up.
2. If you get too far ahead of the army, your soldiers may mistake you for the enemy.
3. Do not complain about the bottom rungs of the ladder; they helped to get you higher.
4. If you want to enjoy the rainbow, be prepared to endure the storm.

ACTIVITY 3 · BATON PASS

Objectives

- Collaborate with team members to find ways to pass the batons
- Contribute to a team goal
- Communicate and cooperate with team members
- Participate in a group conversation to process and evaluate the experience

Preparation

Time: 1 minute

Materials: 1 Toobeez set
         chart paper (optional)

Setup:

1. Provide one 36" Toobeez tube to each participant.

Character Focus

Citizenship

Activity Plan

Group Size: 4 - 8

Time: 15 - 20 minutes

Mental Intensity: 1

Physical Intensity: 1

Space: Medium

The Challenge

The entire group must pass the Toobeez batons simultaneously without dropping them.

Baton Pass

Safety Reminders!

Appropriate caution is important to conduct these activities in a safe manner. Be sure to review these reminders prior to beginning the activity, and if necessary, share reminders with the group during the activity.

- Follow general safety procedures
- If the group attempts the third variation (Toobeez Toss), participants should not use a lot of force when tossing the batons

- A rhythm helps participants to work together. For example, electing a leader to guide the group with a rhythm such as "1, 2, 3, pass…1, 2, 3, pass" is helpful

Activity Instructions

1. Circle up the group, and share the following storyline.

While traveling through the Amazon jungle, your team encounters a village with an unusual custom. On special occasions, the village elders stand in a circle and pass "knowledge batons" around the circle in a highly coordinated way. This custom demonstrates the importance of working together and passing on knowledge to future generations. The village elders have asked your team to demonstrate the baton toss so they can see your level of commitment to teamwork and the sharing of knowledge.

34

Baton Pass

2. Read aloud the following Activity Challenge Box to the group.

> **Challenge:** The entire group must pass the Toobeez batons simultaneously without dropping them. Follow the guidelines below:
> - Participants must stay in one place
> - The Toobeez batons may not fall on the ground
> - Everyone must switch batons simultaneously
> - If any guidelines are broken, the group must begin again

3. To begin the activity, have participants first work through the Problem-Solving Sequence (refer to page 152 for the six sequence steps).

4. In a circle, start by holding batons in a vertical position, standing each baton upright on the floor (refer to the photo). Each person needs to simultaneously exchange batons with the person to their right without dropping them.

5. If participants get stuck, have the students circle up again. Use questions to help guide the group back on track, but do not provide the participants with answers. Allow them to work together.

6. If your group is still struggling OR if you feel your group would benefit from an additional challenge, present a variation provided on the next page.

7. After the activity, move to the "Activity Discussion and Processing" section of the activity.

> See page 6 for available teambuilding training options!

35

Activity Variations

1. Passing variations.
If you started the game by passing batons to the right using your dominant hand, try passing the batons to the left using your non-dominant hand. Another option is to skip a person when passing the batons. Instead of passing the baton directly next to you, skip a person and pass the baton two people away.

2. Add some weight.
Place Toobeez balls on the ends of the tubes to challenge the participants.

3. Try a Toobeez Toss.
Try tossing the baton to the person to the right, to the left, or two people away. Make sure participants toss the batons rather than throw them with force.

Activity Notes

Acknowledgments
This activity was described in a book entitled *The New Games Book* published in 1976. In this book, the activity is called "Lummi Sticks."

Activity Discussion and Processing

Discussion Topic: Working together

A high degree of coordination is required to successfully pass the Toobeez "knowledge" batons. "Coordination" is defined as "operating as a unit." High-functioning teams are extremely coordinated in all aspects of their interactions including leadership, planning, execution, communication and so on.

Questions for Discussion

- On a scale of 1 – 10 (where 1 is poor and 10 is excellent), rate the level of coordination on your team. Where do we want to be on this scale?
- How can your team achieve the desired level of coordination? Have participants name specific action steps. What would life be like when we experience that level of coordination?
- What will life be like if we stay where we are?

Motivator

Discuss the following quotes with the participants.

"You teach best what you most need to learn." - *Richard Bach*

"Give a man a fish and you feed him for a day. Teach him how to fish and you feed him for a lifetime." - *Lao Tzu*

ACTIVITY 4 — CATERPILLAR TRAVERSE

Objectives

- Collaborate with team members to travel as a group through the squares
- Communicate and cooperate with team members
- Participate in a group conversation to process and evaluate the experience

Character Focus

Cooperation

Preparation

Time: 5 minutes
Materials: 4 Toobeez squares
2 boundary ropes
1 bandana per person
chart paper (optional)

Setup:

1. About 20 feet apart, position two boundary ropes on the ground parallel to one another.
2. Create four Toobeez squares and place them within the roped-off area (as pictured). Squares should be about 6" apart.

Activity Plan

Group Size: 5 - 10
Time: 20 – 40 minutes
Mental Intensity: 2
Physical Intensity: 2
Space: Lots

The Challenge

The entire group must travel through the arranged squares as a unit.

38

Caterpillar Traverse

Safety Reminders!

Appropriate caution is important to conduct these activities in a safe manner. Be sure to review these reminders prior to beginning the activity, and if necessary, share reminders with the group during the activity.

- Follow general safety procedures
- People with knee, ankle or back injuries should not participate
- When tying bandanas around ankles, tie them loosely to prevent injury
- The group should move slowly to avoid injuries
- For more suggestions, refer to the "Activity Discussion and Processing" section

- This activity is best for groups that are patient. Do not attempt this activity with an overactive or immature group
- If you have more than ten people, create multiple teams and provide each team with a set of stepping stones

Activity Instructions

1. Circle up the group, and share the following storyline.

> Your team must travel from one side of a canyon to the other. The good news is that tall pillars extend up from the canyon floor providing your team with "stepping stones" from one side of the canyon to the other. The bad news is the wind through the canyon is so powerful that you must cross the canyon connected to each other to avoid being blown away. Get your team to the other side as one group, and you will find success!

39

Caterpillar Traverse

2. Read aloud the following Activity Challenge Box to the group.

> **Challenge:** The entire group must travel through the arranged squares as a unit. Follow the guidelines below:
> - The boundary ropes and stepping stones may not be moved
> - The group must remain in a line with ankles tied throughout the activity
> - Everyone must only step within the Toobeez squares
> - No other equipment may be used
> - If any guidelines are broken, the group must begin again

3. To begin the activity, have participants first work through the Problem-Solving Sequence (refer to page 152 for the six sequence steps).

4. Ask the group to stand behind one of the boundary lines (on one side of the river) and then line up shoulder to shoulder. Provide each person with a bandana, and ask them to loosely tie their ankles together.

5. Be sure to monitor the group for safety as they attempt the activity.

6. If participants get stuck, have the students circle up again. Use questions to help guide the group back on track, but do not provide the participants with answers. Allow them to work together.

7. If your group is still struggling OR if you feel your group would benefit from an additional challenge, present a variation provided on the next page.

8. After the activity, move to the "Activity Discussion and Processing" section of the activity.

40

Caterpillar Traverse

Activity Variations

1. Use a blindfold.
Give a few people a bandana to blindfold themselves for part of the activity.

2. Limit the time.
Provide a time limit (for example, 20 minutes) for the group to complete the task.

3. Create two groups.
Divide the team in half with one group starting on each end. The groups must switch places before time runs out. See if the groups work together or against one another.

Activity Notes

> See page 6 for available teambuilding training options!

> **Acknowledgments**
> I first learned this activity from Steve Thompson.

Caterpillar Traverse

Activity Discussion and Processing

Discussion Topic: Accomplishments

Prior to the activity, ask the group to do the following:

- Identify your dreams and goals, both individually and as a team. Write them down on index cards and place them on a chair on the other side of the "canyon"

- Identify your strengths, skills and attributes both individually and collectively. Write them on index cards and place them in a special bucket or container. The group must carry this bucket with them throughout the activity

Questions for Discussion

- Was the obstacle (the "canyon") easier or harder to get across than what you had originally thought?

- Did you use all the strengths, skills and attributes of your team? Describe. Did you use skills not originally listed? If yes, which ones? When did you use them?

- Are the goals you listed worth the hard effort?

- Would you like to add a new goal or two?

- In this activity, your team was held together by ankle ties. What keeps your group together in real life?

Motivator

In the storyline, your team is traveling across a canyon on "stepping stones." The following quotes all mention the phrase "stepping stones." Read the quotes (one, some or all) and discuss them with your group.

- What are the authors of these quotes saying to you?

"Develop success from failures. Discouragement and failure are two of the surest stepping stones to success." - *Dale Carnegie (1888-1955), American lecturer and author*

"The block of granite which was an obstacle in the pathway of the weak becomes a stepping stone in the pathway of the strong." - *Thomas Carlyle (1795-1881), Scottish historian, essayist and leading figure in the Victorian era*

"Failures to heroic minds are the stepping stones to success." - *Thomas C. Haliburton (1796-1865), Canadian writer*

ACTIVITY 5 ...... CHANNELS ....

Objectives

- Collaborate with team members to create a channel to move the ball
- Communicate with team members
- Work cooperatively as a group
- Participate in a group conversation to process and evaluate the experience

Preparation

Time: 1 minute
Materials: 2 Toobeez tubes per person
1 Toobeez ball
1 bucket
chart paper (optional)

Setup:
1. Provide each person with two tubes of equal length.
2. Place a bucket a distance from where the group will set up.

Character Focus
Communication

Activity Plan

Group Size: 6 - 20

Time: 5 – 25 minutes

Mental Intensity: 1

Physical Intensity: 1

Space: Medium

The Challenge
The entire group must create a channel using the Toobeez to transport a ball into a bucket.

43

Safety Reminders!

Appropriate caution is important to conduct activities in a safe manner. Be sure to review these reminders prior to beginning the activity, and share reminders with the group if necessary.

- Follow general safety procedures

- Encourage groups to start out moving slowly. The "leap frogging" requires timing, communication and focus
- Groups that rush can have an extremely difficult time with this activity

See page 6 for available teambuilding training options!

Activity Instructions

1. Circle up the group, and share the following storyline.

You are a team of disaster relief workers attempting to transport desperately needed food and medicine (in the shape of yellow balls) to a village that needs your help. Your team must find a workable solution for transporting the food and medicine over a great distance.

Channels

2. Read aloud the following Activity Challenge Box to the group.

Challenge: The entire group must create a channel using the Toobeez to transport a ball into a bucket. Follow the guidelines below:
- The ball may not touch anything other than the channels and the bucket
- The channels must remain in the air at all times
- When a ball is in your channel, your feet must remain still
- People may move when the ball is not in their channel
- The ball may not be touched once the activity has begun
- If any guidelines are broken, the group must begin again

---

3. To begin the activity, have participants first work through the Problem-Solving Sequence (refer to page 152 for the six sequence steps).
4. The group will begin at an arbitrary starting point. Set a bucket approximately 30 feet from the group so the group must "leap frog" each other to successfully drop the ball in the bucket. The greater the distance, the harder the challenge.
5. If participants get stuck, have the students circle up again. Use questions to help guide the group back on track, but do not provide the participants with answers. Allow them to work together.
6. If your group is still struggling OR if you feel your group would benefit from an additional challenge, present a variation provided on the next page.
7. After the activity, move to the "Activity Discussion and Processing" section of the activity.

Channels

Activity Variations

1. Allow no participant contact.

Inform participants that they may not physically touch another person's channel, but the channel tubes may touch one another. Also, the ball may only move in a forward direction with no backward rolling.

2. Add an obstacle.

Have the group transport the ball uphill (for example, up a staircase), under/over an obstacle (for example, a desk, tree, etc.), or require the group to use NO verbal communication.

Activity Notes

Acknowledgments
I first learned this activity from master facilitator Viva Pizer.

Activity Discussion and Processing

Discussion Topic: Communication

In this activity, you were attempting to get the ball(s) to "flow" from one point to another.

- Describe the skills you used to make the ball flow easily from one point to another
- Can you use these same skills to help things flow in your group? How?
- What would you like to have flow easier in your group? (Ideas, money, leadership, kindness, etc.)

Discussion Topic: Disaster

If appropriate, discuss disaster relief with your group.

- What is a "disaster?" How is it different than any other kind of tragedy?
- Has anyone ever come to the aid of someone who has experienced some kind of disaster? How? What did it feel like to help? What was the response of the person/people receiving the help?
- Other than basic living necessities such as medical attention, food, shelter, water and clothing, what do people who have experienced a disaster also need?
- What skills can you bring to a real disaster relief situation? Would you like to learn new skills that you could use in a disaster relief situation? If yes, what kind of skills?

Motivator

In the storyline, your team is involved in disaster relief. In the following quotes, disaster is mentioned. Discuss the message these authors are trying to communicate to you.

"Happiness and strength endure only in the absence of hate. To hate alone is the road to **disaster**. To love is the road to strength. To love in spite of all is the secret of greatness. And may very well be the greatest secret in this universe." - *L. Ron Hubbard (1911-1986), American science-fiction writer and novelist*

"I always tried to turn every **disaster** into an opportunity." - *John D. Rockefeller (1839-1937), American industrialist and philanthropist; founder of the Standard Oil Company*

47

ACTIVITY 6 .... CROSSOVER

Objectives

- Collaborate with team members to quickly switch places with other members
- Communicate with the group to synchronize movements
- Work cooperatively to contribute toward a goal
- Participate in a group conversation to process and evaluate the experience

Character Focus
Citizenship

Preparation

Time: 1 minute
Materials: 1 Toobeez square
stopwatch
chart paper (optional)
Setup:
1. Build the Toobeez square and place it on the ground.

Activity Plan

Group Size: 20 - 40
Time: 15 – 30 minutes
Mental Intensity: 2
Physical Intensity: 1
Space: Medium

The Challenge
The entire group must quickly move from one side to the other by switching places with a partner.

Crossover

Safety Reminders!

Appropriate caution is important to conduct these activities in a safe manner. Be sure to review these reminders prior to beginning the activity, and if necessary, share reminders with the group during the activity.

- Follow general safety procedures
- Be sure group members use caution when approaching the square to avoid collisions

- This is a deceptively simple looking activity…until you try it. If you have a group of ten doing this activity, it is relatively simple. However, if you have a group of 15 or 20, watch out! The challenge increases in large groups because participants have greater difficulty sharing ideas
- If you have a group larger than 20 people, split the group into two groups

Activity Instructions

1. Circle up the group, and share the following storyline.

You are each the pilot of your own plane, and you must fly your important cargo to its final destination. It seems that all the planes must fly over a central point in the country. The air traffic controllers are out to lunch, so before you take off, you must devise a plan with the other pilots that will allow you to get to your destination as fast as you can without any collisions.

2. Read aloud the following Activity Challenge Box to the group.

> **Challenge**: The entire group must quickly move from one side to the other by switching places with a partner. Follow the guidelines below:
> - Partners must step into the square at the same time
> - Participants may not touch anyone at any time during this activity (including clothing)
> - Partners must be across from each other at the start and end of the activity
> - The Toobeez square may not be changed
> - If any guidelines are broken, the group must begin again

3. To begin the activity, have participants first work through the Problem-Solving Sequence (refer to page 152 for the six sequence steps).

4. Have the group surround the square. Participants should identify their partner as the person standing directly across from them. The goal is to change places with your partner as quickly as possible. If there are an odd number of people, have a "partnership" form out of a group of three.

5. Time starts when the facilitator says "go" and stops when everyone is finished crossing. The group will be allowed five tries to get the lowest time.

6. Be sure to monitor the group for safety as they attempt the activity.

7. If participants get stuck, have the students circle up again. Use questions to help guide the group back on track, but do not provide the participants with answers. Allow them to work together.

8. If your group is still struggling OR if you feel your group would benefit from an additional challenge, present the variation provided on the next page.

9. After the activity, move to the "Activity Discussion and Processing" section of the activity.

> See page 6 for available teambuilding training options!

Activity Variations

1. Create a small square.
Create a smaller square using the shortest tubes. The short tubes make it much more difficult to touch inside the square simultaneously.

Activity Notes

Acknowledgments
This activity was described by Karl Rhonke
in his book, *Quicksilver.*

Activity Discussion and Processing

Discussion Topic: Improving Yourself
This activity requires the group to look for ways to continually improve.

Discussion Questions
- What does it mean to "continuously improve?"
- Is it really possible to improve forever? Does there ever come a time when improvement is not possible?
- How often is it possible to devise a plan that helps everyone?
- If citizens continue to improve themselves, how does this help and contribute to society?

Motivator
In this activity, you were asked to practice "continuous improvement." The authors below offer their views on improvement.
- What are the following authors saying to you?
- How can you apply their wisdom to your team?

"There is only one corner of the universe you can be certain of **improving**, and that's your own self." - *Aldous Huxley (1894-1963), English novelist and critic*

"Normal fear protects us; abnormal fear paralyzes us. Normal fear motivates us to **improve** our individual and collective welfare; abnormal fear constantly poisons and distorts our inner lives. Our problem is not to be rid of fear, but rather to harness and master it." - *Martin Luther King, Jr. (1929-1968), American Baptist minister and civil-rights leader*

"Guard well your spare moments. They are like uncut diamonds. Discard them and their value will never be known. **Improve** them and they will become the brightest gems in a useful life." - *Ralph Waldo Emerson (1803-1882), American poet, lecturer and essayist*

ACTIVITY (7) ········· THE CUBE ·········

Objectives

- Collaborate with team members to move through the cube in unique ways
- Communicate with the group to complete the activity
- Rely on group members
- Participate in a group conversation to process and evaluate the experience

Character Focus
Trust & Caring

Preparation

Time: 5 minutes
Materials: 1 Toobeez cube
5-gallon bucket
chart paper (optional)
Setup:
2. Create a cube using eight of the 36" tubes and eight of the 16" tubes to create four long tubes (refer to the photograph).
3. Balance the cube on the bucket as pictured.

Activity Plan

Group Size: 5 - 20

Time: 15 – 45 minutes

Mental Intensity: 2

Physical Intensity: 3

Space: Medium

The Challenge
The entire group must work as team to earn points by moving through the cube through unique pathways.

Safety Reminders!

Appropriate caution is important to conduct these activities in a safe manner. Be sure to review these reminders prior to beginning the activity, and if necessary, share reminders with the group during the activity.

- Proper spotting techniques must be reviewed prior to starting this challenge (refer to the "Safety Procedures" section on page 19)
- It is ideal to have cushions or pads placed under the Toobeez structure to minimize the effects of a fall
- All participants must be spotted as they travel through the cube
- If your group is not physically strong enough, mature enough and/or calm enough, do not attempt this activity

Helpful Hints!

- Some groups may want to practice passing people through the cube prior to actually starting. **Note:** Allowing the group to practice on the cube itself can take away some of the unknown aspects of the activity. Consider setting limitations on the practice (time, number of tries, etc.)

See page 6 for available teambuilding training options!

Activity Instructions

1. Circle up the group, and share the following storyline.

> Your team is enrolled in a special NASA training program. The space agency is looking for a team of astronauts to send into space to fix an expensive satellite. The mission will require a team to work in close proximity to each other and the equipment. NASA has devised a challenge for your team that simulates the requirements of the actual space mission. The team must move in and around a model satellite without touching it. If you pass the test, your team will be awarded the real mission!

2. Read aloud the following Activity Challenge Box to the group.

> **Challenge**: The entire group must work as team to earn points by moving through the cube through unique pathways. Follow the guidelines below:
> - Each team member must pass through the cube using a unique pathway. Once a pathway is used, that unique sequence of travel cannot be used again
> - The cube may only be supported by the bucket base, and it may not fall over
> - Anyone traveling through the cube must be spotted
> - Participants may not jump or dive through cube pathways
> - Team members may not be launched through the cube
> - No additional equipment may be used
> - The group *MUST* complete this activity in a safe manner or the activity will be stopped
> - If any guidelines are broken, the group may be given a penalty (see Step #6)

3. Gather the team around the cube and explain the point system.
    One point is earned when passing from a lower hole to a lower hole.
    Two points are earned when passing from a lower hole to an upper hole.
    Three points are earned when passing from an upper hole to an upper hole.

4. To begin the activity, have participants first work through the Problem-Solving Sequence (refer to page 152 for the six sequence steps).

5. Be sure to monitor the group for safety as they attempt the activity.

6. If a touch occurs, choose one of the following penalties: A) everyone starts again, B) only one person has to travel back through, C) the group may not communicate verbally for five minutes, or D) a combination of these.

55

7. If participants get stuck, have the students circle up again. Use questions to help guide the group back on track, but do not provide the participants with answers. Allow them to work together.
8. If your group is still struggling OR if you feel your group would benefit from an additional challenge, present a variation provided below.
9. After the activity, move to the "Activity Discussion and Processing" section of the activity.

Activity Variations

1. **Add an obstacle.**

Hang a string from the top center of the cube (about 24" long). The team may not touch the string during the activity.

2. **Hang the cube.**

Instead of balancing the cube, hang the cube from something (for example, a tree limb). Ask the group to travel through the cube as described in the rules.

Activity Notes

Acknowledgments
I first learned this activity from Jim Cain who co-authored *Teamwork & Teamplay*. Jim credits Earl LeBlanc with the creation of this activity.

www.project-connect.net   www.TeachMeTeamwork.com

The Cube

Activity Discussion and Processing

Discussion Topic: Trusting One Another

In this storyline, you were to imagine yourself as a team of astronauts in space working on a satellite. This would be a dangerous and challenging mission.

- Use your imagination. In what type of rescue mission would you like to see your team involved?
- What new skills would you need to learn to successfully complete the rescue mission?

Discussion Questions

- What role did trust play in this activity?
- Who did you trust?
- At what level did you trust them? Rate your team on a scale from 1 – 10 (where 1 means you do not trust them at all and 10 means you trust them a lot)

Motivator

In the storyline, you have an opportunity to be selected for a mission in outer space. Teachers throughout the ages have studied and written about our life's mission. In the quotes below, the word "mission" is mentioned.

- What are these authors saying to you?

"To succeed in your **mission**, you must have single-minded devotion to your goal."
- Abdul Kalam (born 1931), President of India

"When you discover your **mission**, you will feel its demand. It will fill you with enthusiasm and a burning desire to get to work on it." *- W. Clement Stone (1902-2002), American best-selling author and founder of Combined Insurance Co. (now a part of Aon Corp.)*

"Everyone has his own specific vocation or **mission** in life; everyone must carry out a concrete assignment that demands fulfillment. Therein he cannot be replaced, nor can his life be repeated, thus, everyone's task is unique as his specific opportunity."
- Viktor Frankl (1905-1997), Austrian psychiatrist and psychotherapist

ACTIVITY 8 FOGGY BRIDGE BUILDING

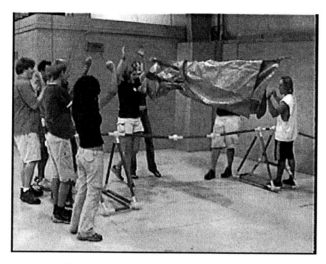

Objectives

- Cooperate with team members to build a bridge that connects with the other team's bridge
- Use communication and listening skills actively
- Participate in a group conversation to process and evaluate the experience

Preparation

Time: 5 minutes

Materials: 1 Toobeez set (divide pieces equally between the teams)
1 tarp or curtain
chart paper (optional)

Setup:
1. Divide the Toobeez, giving half to each team.
2. Hang up a large opaque tarp or blanket. On each side, measure out from the curtain the length of one long and one short Toobeez tube. Mark with masking tape (as pictured here to the right).

The Challenge

Two bridge-building teams must build their portion of the bridge so that when the curtain is removed, one Toobeez tube can be added to form one bridge.

Character Focus

Communication

Activity Plan

Group Size: 2 – 5/team

Time: 20 – 55 minutes

Mental Intensity: 3

Physical Intensity: 1

Space: Medium

58

Foggy Bridge Building

<u>Safety Reminders!</u>

Appropriate caution is important to conduct these activities in a safe manner. Be sure to review these reminders prior to beginning the activity, and if necessary, share reminders with the group during the activity.

- Follow general safety procedures

- This is an advanced activity that requires an amazing amount of clear communication and patience between the two bridge-building teams
- If you have a sophisticated group, this activity will likely provide them with a great deal of information, which is worth discussing and analyzing. Be prepared to discuss non-success because this is common
- This activity pushes groups that have not been working well together to find some common ground
- It does not matter if the two structures the groups build match in design. What does matter is that the final piece fits into place

<u>Activity Instructions</u>

1. Circle up the group, and share the following storyline.

> For as long as most people could remember, the governments of two countries separated by a river did not trust each other. Each government had spread false accusations and rumors for years, causing great tension between the nations. To complicate matters, a thick fog laid upon the river like a giant curtain, and the people of both countries could not see through the fog. One day, visionary leaders from both countries decided on a magnificent plan to build a bridge through the fog in order to establish harmony and unity between the peoples of the two nations. Your team has been challenged with building the bridge through the fog to unite these two countries.

Foggy Bridge Building

2. Read aloud the following Activity Challenge Box to the group.

> **Challenge**: Two bridge-building teams must build their portion of the bridge so that when the curtain is removed, one Toobeez tube can be added to form one bridge. Follow the guidelines below:
> * No bridge supports can be used on the ground between the tape and the curtain
> * Teams can not look on the other side of the curtain
> * Nothing may touch or move the curtain
> * Team members are only allowed to communicate <u>verbally</u>
> * The tape and the curtain may not be altered
> * If any guidelines are broken, the group must begin again

3. Explain to the team that the curtain represents the fog that plagues this bridge-building effort, and the tape represents the riverbank.
4. To begin the activity, have participants first work through the Problem-Solving Sequence (refer to page 152 for the six sequence steps).
5. Teams should arrange themselves on opposite sides of the curtain.
6. There is no predetermined structure. That is, groups do not have to build the structure like the one pictured in this guide. Also, it does not matter if the groups build matching structures. What does matter is that the groups communicate to ensure the final piece fits into place.
7. If participants get stuck, have the students circle up again. Use questions to help guide the group back on track, but do not provide the participants with answers. Allow them to work together.
8. If your group is still struggling OR if you feel your group would benefit from an additional challenge, present the variation provided on the next page.

Foggy Bridge Building

9. When time is up, the curtain will be pulled away and the teams will be given one opportunity to insert (place) one piece of Toobeez into the two bridge sections, thus completing the bridge.

10. After the activity, move to the "Activity Discussion and Processing" section of the activity.

> See page 6 for available teambuilding training options!

Activity Variations

1. Test the bridge's strength.

Once the final piece is inserted to finish the bridge, test it to see how strong it is (how much weight it can hold).

Activity Notes

Acknowledgments
I first learned this activity from master facilitator Viva Pizer.

Activity Discussion and Processing

Discussion Topic: The importance of vision
In the storyline, you are a team of bridge builders described as having a "vision."
- What does it mean to have a "vision" of something?
- Martin Luther King, the great civil rights leader, once gave a speech in which he said, "I have a dream…" Is a dream the same as a vision?

Discussion Topic: Cooperation
In the storyline, you find out that a "thick fog" lays on top of the river "like a giant curtain" separating two groups of people.
- What can separate people in real life?
- What can bring people together?
- Should two groups of people ever remain separated?
- What strengthens the feeling of team and unity in our own group?
- Is there anything that causes separation in our own group?

Motivator
In the storyline, you were asked to build a bridge through a fog. The fog is a metaphor for all that can cloud our judgment. In the quotes below, some famous thinkers offer their insights in regards to this notion of "fog."

"The best ammunition against lies is the truth, there is no ammunition against gossip. It is like a **fog** and the clear wind blows it away and the sun burns it off." - *Ernest Hemingway (1899-1961), American novelist and short-story writer; awarded the Nobel Prize for Literature in 1954*

"Technology is so much fun but we can drown in our technology. The **fog** of information can drive out knowledge." - *Daniel J. Boorstin (born 1914), American social historian and educator; awarded the Pulitzer Prize in history in 1974*

"Truth is the torch that gleams through the **fog** without dispelling it."
- *Claude Adrien Helvetius (1715-1771), French philosopher*

ACTIVITY 9

HELIUM STICK

Preparation

Time: 1 minute
Materials: 1 long Toobeez tube
                chart paper (optional)
Setup:
1. Have the Toobeez ready.

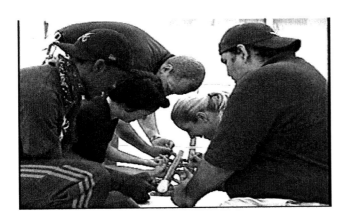

Objectives

- Cooperate with team members to lower the helium stick together
- Communicate with the team to synchronize movements
- Work cooperatively toward a common goal
- Participate in a group conversation to process and evaluate the experience

Character Focus
Teamwork

Activity Plan

Group Size: 6

Time: 40 – 60 minutes

Mental Intensity: 3+

Physical Intensity: 1

Space: Minimal

The Challenge
Lower the Toobeez tube to the ground.

63

Helium Stick

Safety Reminders!

Appropriate caution is important to conduct these activities in a safe manner. Be sure to review these reminders prior to beginning the activity, and if necessary, share reminders with the group during the activity.

> • Follow general safety procedures

> • Do not attempt this challenging activity with groups in serious conflict
> • This is an intense communication activity where each person must be absolutely committed to doing his or her part. People are likely to get frustrated, and it is common for some blaming to occur
> • It is common to lose contact with the tube multiple times. If this happens to a group you are working with, you have been given a great opportunity to talk about the level of commitment to (1) the task, and (2) following instructions

Activity Instructions

1. Prior to leading the activity, ask the group to identify either their team goals or their team vision. Have the group write them on masking tape. Attach the tape to the Toobeez pipe. This will setup the metaphor of identifying goals (or mission) and for making goals happen.
2. Circle up the group, and share the following storyline.

> The government has created a brand new plane designed to measure weather patterns. Your team was assigned to the flight, which took you so high above the earth's surface that you are now weightless. Suddenly the pilot announces an emergency. A fuel line has broken and must be replaced so the plane can land safely before you run out of fuel. Your team must delicately return the pipe section to its proper place to finish the repair. It is a tricky repair that requires the entire team.

3. Read aloud the following Activity Challenge Box to the group.

> **Challenge**: Lower the Toobeez tube to the ground. Follow the guidelines below:
> - The tube's starting position is at waist level
> - The tops of both index fingers must be placed below the tube
> - *Only* the tops of the index fingers can touch the tube
> - Nothing else is allowed to touch the tube
> - No one may loose contact with the tube at any time
> - If any guidelines are broken, the group must begin again

4. To begin the activity, have participants first work through the Problem-Solving Sequence (refer to page 152 for the six sequence steps).

5. Divide your group in half and have them create two parallel lines facing each other (approximately 12" – 18" apart). The participants should stand shoulder to shoulder, holding out their index fingers at waist level.

6. Place a Toobeez tube on top of their fingers. *IMPORTANT: Place the tube on their fingers from behind and in the middle of one of the lines. Keep your hand on top of the tube to prevent the group from raising the tube.

7. With your hand still on the tube, read the following directions: "As a group, you must lower this tube to the ground without even a single person on the team losing contact with the tube. Should someone lose contact with the tube, you must start again."

8. Release your hand from the tube. Here is what typically happens in this activity: When you release the tube, the group will often RAISE the tube (not lower it)! It is likely to take several attempts to just keep the tube steady. You may have to stop this activity several times mid-stream to help the group.

9. If participants get stuck, have the students circle up again. Use questions to help guide the group back on track, but do not provide the participants with answers. Allow them to work together.

10. If your group is still struggling OR if you feel your group would benefit from an additional challenge, present a variation provided on the next page.

11. After the activity, move to the "Activity Discussion and Processing" section of the activity.

Activity Variations

1. Increasing the difficulty: More people and a longer helium stick.
One tube can easily accommodate a team of six people. If you have more people, make a longer tube by connecting another length of tube. This addition makes the activity harder.

2. Building up to this activity: Making it a little bit easier.
Have people pair up with a long tube. Have each pair lower their tube to the ground so they can experience success. Then have the pairs join another pair to form groups of four and repeat the activity. Keep increasing the group size until you have everyone working on one long tube.

See page 6 for available teambuilding training options!

Activity Notes

Acknowledgments
I first learned this activity from Beau Hughes of Hughes Consulting, Inc.

Activity Discussion and Processing

Discussion Topic: Team Goals

It is one thing to write out goals, and it is an entirely other thing to make them happen (or to realize them) as a team.

- What does it take to make our group goals a reality?
- What specific skills were required to lower the Toobeez pipe to the ground?
- Can we use these same skills to make our goals in real life a reality?

True Story from the Author:

I used this activity to help the leadership of an organization realize that having a company vision is one thing and making it a reality is another. I did this by leading the group in a four-hour company vision statement workshop. The tube represented the company vision, and by successfully lowering it to the ground, they could achieve their vision.

What happened next was amazing! When the group began, the tube immediately went in the OPPOSITE direction from where they were trying to go – it went UP! After 50 minutes of trying to lower the tube to the ground, they finally succeeded. I asked the group if they experienced any parallels to real life while doing this activity. "YES!" they said. Everyone had to be committed to the path toward success, and blaming and excuses only served as obstacles on this path. They realized that staying calm and focused was critical.

Motivator

In the storyline, your team is working to repair a broken fuel line. The fuel in this story represents anything positive that keeps us moving forward. Discuss the quotes below.

- What can you learn about "fuel" that is applicable to your life and your team?

"I am building a fire, and everyday I train, I add more **fuel**. At just the right moment, I light the match." - *Mia Hamm (born 1972), American female soccer player*

"Without inspiration the best powers of the mind remain dormant, there is a **fuel** in us which needs to be ignited with sparks." - *Johann Gottfried Von Herder (1744-1803), German poet, critic, theologian and philosopher*

ACTIVITY 10

HOOP PASS

Objectives

- Collaborate with team members to move the hoop around the group
- Use communication and cooperation skills to work as a team
- Participate in a group conversation to process and evaluate the experience

Preparation

Time: 5 minutes
Materials: 1 Toobeez hoop
             chart paper (optional)
Setup:
1. Create a square of Toobeez out of four 24" tubes. An easier version uses the 36" tubes.

Character Focus
Teamwork

Activity Plan

Group Size: 5 - 20

Time: 15 – 45 minutes

Mental Intensity: 2

Physical Intensity: 3

Space: Medium

The Challenge
Pass the Toobeez square around a group as quickly as possible.

Hoop Pass

Safety Reminders!

Appropriate caution is important to conduct activities in a safe manner. Be sure to review these reminders prior to beginning the activity, and share reminders with the group if necessary.

- Follow general safety procedures
- Remove glasses prior to beginning this activity
- Remove high heels prior to beginning this activity

- If you have more than 12 people, consider creating two smaller groups
- Initially a group may find this challenge impossible to complete. Participants might ask, "How do you pass the hoop around the circle without letting go of hands?" This activity will often get a group laughing as they watch each person pass through the hoop
- This is not a good activity for people who are obese or who have difficulty balancing

Activity Instructions

1. Circle up the group, and share the following storyline.

> You are members of a cave rescue team. As everyone knows, cave rescue requires a team to act quickly and efficiently to successfully save an injured victim. The Toobeez square represents the size of the cave tunnels within which your team must learn to perform rescues. Everyone must get through the make-believe cave opening with speed and efficiency.

69

Hoop Pass

2. Read aloud the following Activity Challenge Box to the group.

> **Challenge**: Pass the Toobeez square around a group as quickly as possible. Follow the guidelines below:
> - The hoop (square) must travel in a clockwise direction
> - No letting go of hands
> - Everyone must stand in one location (no running around)
> - If any guidelines are broken, the group must begin again

3. To begin the activity, have participants first work through the Problem-Solving Sequence (refer to page 152 for the six sequence steps).
4. With the group standing in a circle and holding hands, have one pair of people break hands, reach through the hoop (square) and then reconnect hands.
5. Participants should now move the hoop in a clockwise direction.
6. If participants get stuck, have the students circle up again. Use questions to help guide the group back on track, but do not provide the participants with answers. Allow them to work together.
7. If your group is still struggling OR if you feel your group would benefit from an additional challenge, present a variation provided on the next page.
8. After the activity, move to the "Activity Discussion and Processing" section of the activity.

See page 6 for available teambuilding training options!

70

Activity Variations

1. Create two hoops.

To increase the challenge, create two hoops (squares) - one large and one small. Start them in the same location, but ask the group to pass the large hoop in a clockwise direction and the small hoop in a counter-clockwise direction. When the two hoops meet, there is usually some confusion.

2. Timing the group.

Time the group as they pass the hoop to see how long it takes them to get the hoop all the way around. Then, allow the participants another attempt to break the record.

Activity Notes

Acknowledgments
Karl Rohnke provided a description of this activity in his book, *Silver Bullets,* published in 1984. He called the activity "Circle the Circle."

Activity Discussion and Processing

Discussion Topic: Facing life's obstacles

In the storyline, you were asked to get your team through a small space. Accomplishing this task quickly and without errors requires greater skills than getting through slowly. The hoop in this activity could metaphorically represent hoops people jump through on a regular basis (for one reason or another).

- What are some actual hoops in your life through which you have jumped?
- Are hoops good or bad?
- Do some people have more to deal with than others? If so, why?
- What hoops would you add to or remove from your life if you could?

Discussion Questions

- Compare the skills (both individual and team) needed to get through the small opening quickly as opposed to slowly
- Did you help each other get through the opening? How?
- Is it possible to help someone but in the process actually slow them down?
- How do you know when to help someone in real life?

Motivator

In the storyline, your team is practicing to rescue people. One author describes an "irresistible power" which comes to the rescue of people who choose to respond to discouraging situations.

- What is this "power" to which the author is referring?

"What we do not see, what most of us never suspect of existing, is the silent but irresistible power which comes to the rescue of those who fight on with the face of discouragement." - *Napoleon Hill (1883-1970), American author*

ACTIVITY 11 — LONGEST BRIDGE

Objectives

- Collaborate with team members to build the longest bridge possible
- Work cooperatively as a team
- Communicate and listen to the ideas of others
- Participate in a group conversation to process and evaluate the experience

Preparation

Time: 1 minute

Materials: 1 Toobeez set per team
rope or masking tape
chart paper (optional)

Setup:

1. Create one side of a pretend "riverbank" by laying down a long rope on the ground or by applying a piece of masking tape to the ground. This is the side of the river where each group will start building their bridge.

Character Focus

Cooperation

Activity Plan

Group Size: 2 - 5/team

Time: 15 – 45 minutes

Mental Intensity: 2

Physical Intensity: 1

Space: Lots

See page 6 for available teambuilding training options!

The Challenge

Build the longest bridge possible.

Longest Bridge

Safety Reminders!

Appropriate caution is important to conduct these activities in a safe manner. Be sure to review these reminders prior to beginning the activity, and if necessary, share reminders with the group during the activity.

> • Follow general safety procedures

> • Do not rush this activity. Provide at least 15 minutes for the teams to build a bridge. When groups are rushed, they tend to build sloppy bridges that fall over
> • Building bridges is a great metaphor for life. A bridge helps connect people and resources

Activity Instructions

1. Circle up the group, and share the following storyline.

> An eccentric billionaire has run the following ad in your local newspaper: "What our country needs are people with a vision. The vision must be bold and exciting in order to energize and motivate our community. I am looking for a team of people to create such a vision. To find the best team for the job, I have invented the following challenge. The team that builds the longest bridge (from where we are now to where we want to be) will win the challenge. This will prove to me that your team is the one to lead our community into the future."

Longest Bridge

2. Read aloud the following Activity Challenge Box to the group.

> **Challenge**: Build the longest bridge possible. Follow the guidelines below:
> - The length of the bridge will be measured from the riverbank to the closest bridge support. The team with the greatest measurement wins
> - Only the Toobeez can be used to construct the bridge
> - The bridge must span from one riverbank (from the starting side) to a distance out from the riverbank
> - The bridge must be perpendicular to the riverbank
> - The bridge must be free-standing
> - If any guidelines are broken, the group must begin again

3. To begin the activity, have participants first work through the Problem-Solving Sequence (refer to page 152 for the six sequence steps).
4. If participants get stuck, have the students circle up again. Use questions to help guide the group back on track, but do not provide the participants with answers. Allow them to work together.
5. If your group is still struggling OR if you feel your group would benefit from an additional challenge, present the variation provided on the next page.
6. After the activity, move to the "Activity Discussion and Processing" section of the activity.

75

Activity Variations

1. A boat passing under.
Tell the group that a "boat" must be able to pass under the bridge AND the bridge must support one pound of weight at the center of the bridge (without collapsing). Make a boat out of a cardboard box (the taller the box, the harder it will be for the group). Allow the group to view, but not test, the box while they are building.

Activity Notes

Acknowledgments
I first learned this activity from Jim Cain,
co-author of *Teamwork & Teamplay*.

Activity Discussion and Processing

Discussion Topic: Connecting with others
Building a bridge is the perfect metaphor for setting an intention (setting a goal and a vision) and then taking action to experience your intention.

Discussion Questions
- People build bridges to connect people and valuable resources (other people, places, things, etc.). What is a resource your team needs to experience a greater level of success?
- In this activity, your bridge-building supplies consisted of Toobeez. What supplies or resources do you need to experience a greater level of team success?
- Some people say, "Do not burn your bridges." What do they mean by this?

Motivators
The following quotes all mention the word "bridge." Read the quotes (one, some or all), and discuss them with your group.
- What are the authors of these quotes really saying?
- Why do they use the word "bridge?"

"We build too many walls and not enough bridges." - *Isaac Newton (1642-1727), English mathematician and physicist; "Father of modern science"*

"Discipline is the bridge between goals and accomplishment." - *Jim Rohn, author and speaker*

"Sometimes, if you stand on the bottom rail of a bridge and lean over to watch the river slipping slowly away beneath you, you will suddenly know everything there is to be known." - *Winnie the Pooh*

"I am where I am because of the bridges that I crossed. Sojourner Truth was a bridge. Harriet Tubman was a bridge. Ida B. Wells was a bridge. Madame C.J. Walker was a bridge. Fannie Lou Hamer was a bridge." - *Oprah Winfrey, American television personality, actress and producer*

77

ACTIVITY 12

MAZE

Objectives

- Collaborate with team members to move all members through the maze
- Work cooperatively and communicate with team members
- Listen to and follow instructions
- Rely on team members
- Participate in a group conversation to process and evaluate the experience

Preparation

Time: 5 minutes

Materials: 1 Toobeez set
selected Maze Map
chart paper (optional)

Setup:
1. Select the "Maze Map" (answer key) you plan to use with the group. Samples are provided on pages 82-83.
2. Build a Toobeez maze. Use the photos or Multimedia Training CD as a guide.

Character Focus

Trust & Communication

Activity Plan

Group Size: 5 - 20

Time: 15 – 45 minutes

Mental Intensity: 2

Physical Intensity: 3

Space: Medium

The Challenge

The team must successfully solve the established (but hidden) maze route and get as many team members through the maze before time runs out.

Maze

Safety Reminders!

Appropriate caution is important to conduct these activities in a safe manner. Be sure to review these reminders prior to beginning the activity, and if necessary, share reminders with the group during the activity.

* Follow general safety procedures

* When presenting this activity, you can choose to read the directions to the group OR you can supply them with a copy of the written directions. Older teens do well with the latter option
* With younger participants, you may need to help them work through the directions rule by rule so they have a clear understanding. This may take 10 - 15 minutes
* The best place for the facilitator during this activity is at the end of the maze, opposite to where the participants start
* Consider having an assistant (another teacher) whose job it is to operate the Maze Map. This frees up the primary facilitator to observe the group's dynamics

Activity Instructions

1. Circle up the group, and share the following storyline.

> A mysterious disease has broken out which can only be cured using a plant that is now extinct. A secret government agency has built a time travel machine, and they have sent your team back in time to retrieve a sample of the needed plant. To get back to the current time and to save thousands of people from this terrible disease, your team must travel through a "time grid" (time maze) together. Time is running out. Get your team through the maze to help save thousands of people.

79

Maze

2. Read aloud the following Activity Challenge Box to the group.

> **Challenge**: The team must successfully solve the established (but hidden) maze route and get as many team members through the maze before time runs out. Follow the guidelines below:
> - The group may talk during the planning phases, but once people enter the maze, only non-verbal communication (such as pointing) is allowed
> - The participants must never see the Maze Map (answer key)
> - Only one person is allowed in the maze at a time
> - Team members may keep mental records of the route (but no marking of the route or maps)
> - The team has 25 minutes to complete the activity
> - If any guidelines are broken, the group may be penalized

3. To begin the activity, have participants first work through the Problem-Solving Sequence (refer to page 152 for the six sequence steps).

4. Have the group gather at one end of the maze. Explain that there is one route through the maze, and the facilitator has a "map" of the route.

5. Everyone must begin and end the maze at the areas specified by the facilitator. The group must establish a sequence, and each person must attempt the route in the established order. After each person has made an attempt, the order starts over.

6. As team members move through the maze, the facilitator will match their movements with those of the answer key. If a participant steps in the wrong space, the facilitator will "BEEP" that person. The person who was "beeped" must get off the maze, return to the end of the line and let the next person go. The beeped person goes again when it is their turn.

7. Once someone makes it through the maze successfully, they should focus on helping everyone else get through.

8. If participants get stuck, have the students circle up again. Use questions to help guide the group back on track, but do not provide the participants with answers. Allow them to work together.

9. If your group is still struggling OR if you feel your group would benefit from an additional challenge, present a variation provided below.

10. After the activity, move to the "Activity Discussion and Processing" section of the activity.

See page 6 for available teambuilding training options!

Activity Variations

1. Make the activity easier.
One way to make this activity easier is to allow the group to talk freely if they all move away from the maze and meet in a "special" meeting area (for example, inside a rope circle) while the clock is stopped. Doing this encourages problem solving and sharing of ideas.

2. Make the activity more challenging.
You can vary the difficulty by decreasing the amount of time (less time = harder).

Activity Notes

Acknowledgments
I first learned this activity from master facilitator Viva Pizer.

A Note About Selecting Your Map
You can increase the difficulty by using a higher number "Maze Answer Key Map." The higher the map number, the harder the maze. As a point of reference, a group of ten-year-olds can solve Maze Map #1 in approximately 25 minutes. Use the blank Maze Map to create your own maps.

Blank Map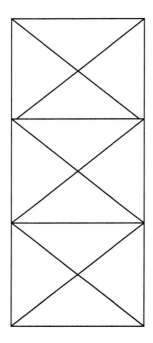

Maze Map #1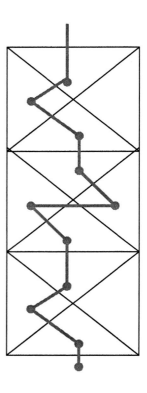

Maze

Maze Map # 2

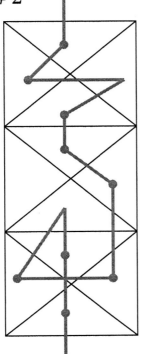

Maze Map # 3

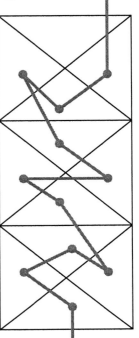

Maze Map # 4

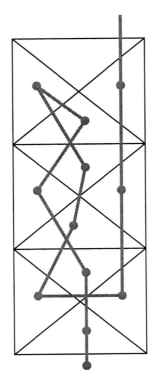

www.project-connect.net

www.TeachMeTeamwork.com

Activity Discussion and Processing

Discussion Topic: Trust

Some students are reluctant to either give or receive help, so this activity can start a great conversation around the topic of trusting and helping others.

Discussion Questions

- Who received help from others during the activity? Who gave help?
- Who did you trust to give you information and advice during this activity?
- Did anyone receive advice (directions) that led him or her to make an incorrect move?
- How do you know who to trust in the real world?
- What criteria do you have in order to trust someone?

Discussion Topic: Problem Solving

The maze activity provides many opportunities to explore how the team worked together to solve a problem.

Discussion Questions

- Who solved the maze? (This is a tricky question. This does not ask who the first person through the maze was, yet some groups see the first person through as the person who "solved" the puzzle. In fact, the reality is it took everyone's effort to get the first person through)
- Who made a mistake during this activity? (Everyone will make a mistake at some point during this activity. When everyone acknowledges that they have all made mistakes, point out that they were still able to solve the challenge, if in fact they were able to learn from their mistakes)
- When are mistakes "good" or "bad?" (Generally groups will say that mistakes are good when you pay attention to them and do not repeat them, and they are bad when the same mistake is repeated over and over again)
- What would you like to change if you really could travel back in time?

(continued on the next page)

Maze

Motivators

The storyline in this activity describes a "disease" that must be cured. The following quotes offer some insights into disease.

- What are the authors of these quotes really saying?

"Every human being is the author of his own health or disease."
- *Buddha Hindu Prince Gautama Siddharta (563 – 483 B.C.), founder of Buddhism*

"The biggest disease today is not leprosy or tuberculosis, but rather the feeling of being unwanted." - *Mother Teresa of Calcutta (1910-1997), Albanian-born Indian missionary and founder of the Order of the Missionaries of Charity; awarded the Nobel Prize for Peace in 1979*

See page 6 for available teambuilding training options!

85

ACTIVITY
(13) .... MINEFIELD ....

Objectives

- Collaborate with team members to move members through the minefield
- Work cooperatively and communicate with team members
- Listen to and follow instructions
- Rely on team members
- Participate in a group conversation to process and evaluate the experience

Preparation

Time: 5 minutes
Materials: 1 Toobeez set
                70 feet of rope
                chart paper (optional)

Setup:
1. Outline an area with the rope to create a playing area. Make the edges "wavy" to prevent the participants from following the edge of the rope as a potential path.
2. Spread out all Toobeez pieces inside the roped area.

Character Focus
Trust & Perseverance

Activity Plan

Group Size: 4 - 30

Time: 25 – 45 minutes

Mental Intensity: 2

Physical Intensity: 1

Space: Lots

The Challenge
Help your partner successfully travel from one end of the swamp to the other.

86

Safety Reminders!

Appropriate caution is important to conduct these activities in a safe manner. Be sure to review these reminders prior to beginning the activity, and if necessary, share reminders with the group during the activity.

- Follow general safety procedures
- Some people lose their balance when their eyes are closed. If someone begins to lose their balance, they should open their eyes

- During the activity, you may find the group has located an "easy" pathway. Allow yourself the option as the facilitator to adjust the minefield playing area midstream by rearranging the Toobeez pieces. If the group challenges this, remind them you are attempting to mimic real life (that is, things change and you deal with it)
- The great thing about this activity is people work in pairs and are somewhat independent of the other people. Therefore, this is a wonderful activity to use to practice coaching since this activity provides ample opportunities to practice clear and precise communication

Activity Instructions

1. Circle up the group, and share the following storyline.

> Your team must travel through an alligator-infested swamp. So far, you have been able to avoid the alligators by walking on the ground. You have one more section of the swamp to travel through, and you must walk through knee-deep water. Alligators (the Toobeez pieces) are spread out all over and sleeping under the water. Due to the gases in the swamp water that could damage your eyes, people walking through the water must keep their eyes closed. Your partner will help you get through by guiding you around the alligators.

87

Minefield

2. Read aloud the following Activity Challenge Box to the group.

> **Challenge:** Help your partner successfully travel from one end of the swamp to the other. Follow the guidelines below:
> - When one partner is inside the swamp, the other must remain on the outside along the edge
> - People traveling through the swamp must keep their eyes closed and may not be guided through with the use of anything (that is, no holding hands, etc.)
> - If anyone touches an alligator (Toobeez piece) or the rope perimeter, they must return to the starting area and switch with their partner
> - The participants may not alter the playing area
> - If any guidelines are broken, the group must begin again

3. To begin the activity, have participants first work through the Problem-Solving Sequence (refer to page 152 for the six sequence steps).
4. When ready to begin, each pair must start at the designated starting area (one end of the rope rectangle). Each pair will then work through the swamp.
5. Be sure to monitor the group for safety as they attempt the activity.
6. If participants get stuck, have the students circle up again. Use questions to help guide the group back on track, but do not provide the participants with answers. Allow them to work together.
7. If your group is still struggling OR if you feel your group would benefit from an additional challenge, present a variation provided on the next page.
8. After the activity, move to the "Activity Discussion and Processing" section of the activity.

88

Activity Variations

1. Adding obstacles.

Consider making 3-D obstacles out of the Toobeez (rather than laying them all flat on the ground) so team members traveling through the swamp will have to step over or under some things.

2. Create goal cards.

Have participants write down goals on index cards. These cards can be used as the objects this group retrieves from the other end of the swamp.

3. Take away verbal communication.

Do not allow participants to use verbal communication to work through the swamp.

Activity Notes

See page 6 for available teambuilding training options!

Acknowledgments

I was taught this activity by Jeff Long. Karl Rohnke provided a description of this activity in his book, *Silver Bullets,* published in 1984.

Minefield

Activity Discussion and Processing

Discussion Topic: Overcoming obstacles

The alligators in this activity symbolize metaphoric problems the group faces either personally or as a team. Obstacles, like landmines in a minefield, are everywhere in life. Some landmines are big and some are small, but they all do damage when we hit them.

Discussion Questions

- Life is full of obstacles. Some people allow obstacles to prevent them from succeeding. Others keep running into the obstacles. What are the obstacles in your life that you are choosing to avoid?

- We can go through life trying to avoid the obstacles, but it is easier when we have help. Where do you get help in real life? Are you effective at asking for help? Are you good at accepting help? How do you know? Are you good at giving help? How do you know?

- Is it possible to live a life free of obstacles?

Motivators

In this activity, you had to avoid "obstacles" in your path as you worked together to achieve success. The following quotes all mention the word "obstacles." Discuss the quotes.

"A hero is an ordinary individual who finds the strength to persevere and endure in spite of overwhelming obstacles." - *Christopher Reeve (1952 – 2004), American actor, film director and activist*

"Every noble work is bound to face problems and obstacles. It is important to check your goal and motivation thoroughly. One should be very truthful, honest and reasonable. One's actions should be good for others and for oneself as well. Once a positive goal is chosen, you should decide to pursue it all the way to the end. Even if it is not realized, at least there will be no regret." - *Dalai Lama, Head of the Dge-lugs-pa order of Tibetan Buddhist; awarded the Nobel Peace Prize in 1989*

"Enthusiasm releases the drive to carry you over obstacles and adds significance to all you do." - *Norman Vincent Peal (1898-1993), American Protestant clergyman and writer*

ACTIVITY 14 — MIRROR AND MATCH

Objectives

- Collaborate with team members to build the same structure as the other team
- Work cooperatively between teams
- Communicate and listen to the ideas of others
- Participate in a group conversation to process and evaluate the experience

Preparation

Time: 5 minutes

Materials: 1 Toobeez set
1 tarp or curtain
chart paper (optional)

Setup:

1. Hang a large, opaque tarp between the teams.
2. Divide the Toobeez set evenly between the two teams.

Character Focus

Communication

Activity Plan

Group Size: 2 – 5/team

Time: 15 – 55 minutes

Mental Intensity: 3

Physical Intensity: 1

Space: Medium

The Challenge

The two teams, separated by a curtain, must build the exact same structure.

91

Mirror and Match

Safety Reminders!

Appropriate caution is important to conduct activities in a safe manner. Be sure to review these reminders prior to beginning the activity, and share reminders with the group if necessary.

• Follow general safety procedures

• This activity is similar to Activity #8: Foggy Bridge Building found in this guide. This activity, however, is slightly easier • There is a LOT of talking in this activity • This activity requires a great deal of clear communication and patience. For additional information, refer to the "Activity Discussion and Processing" section

Activity Instructions

1. Circle up the group, and share the following storyline.

A team of astronauts is inside the space station, while another team is trapped outside of the space station because of a jammed door. Time is running out. To get the door open, both teams must build identical "keys" (structures).

92

Mirror and Match

2. Read aloud the following Activity Challenge Box to the group.

> **Challenge**: The two teams, separated by a curtain, must build the exact same structure. Follow the guidelines below:
> - Teams must use all Toobeez pieces
> - While the curtain is up, teams are not allowed to look at each other or each other's Toobeez structures
> - Nothing may touch or move the curtain
> - Participants are only allowed to communicate verbally
> - Colors of tubes do not have to match
> - If any guidelines are broken, the group must begin again

3. To begin the activity, have participants first work through the Problem-Solving Sequence (refer to page 152 for the six sequence steps).

4. Through communication, the groups will build matching structures. There is no predetermined structure. That is, groups do not have to build the structure like the one pictured in this guide.

5. If participants get stuck, have the students circle up again. Use questions to help guide the group back on track, but do not provide the participants with answers. Allow them to work together.

6. If your group is still struggling OR if you feel your group would benefit from an additional challenge, present the variation provided on the next page.

7. When time is up, remove the curtain. The two structures must be identical in shape and form. Again, colors of tubes do not have to match.

8. After the activity, move to the "Activity Discussion and Processing" section of the activity.

See page 6 for available teambuilding training options!

93

Activity Variations

1. Encouraging more communication.

Often times, there will be one or two key people on a team that end up doing most of the communicating. Consider asking these people to "take a vacation" for five minutes (a required leave of absence). This will require others to step up.

Activity Notes

Acknowledgments

I developed this activity while working at the YMCA in the early 1980s.

Mirror and Match

Activity Discussion and Processing

Discussion Topic: Communicating for success

This activity requires a great deal of clear communication and patience. It is unlikely the group will achieve success by being lucky. They will most likely have to create a system that they all understand, otherwise too much will be left to guess work (guessing is common in the activity). If you see the group relying on guessing, I encourage you to ask and/or challenge the group about this type of behavior.

Discussion Questions

- Define "communication." How do you know when two people have communicated?
- Define "clear communication." How do you know when two people have clearly communicated?
- Define "successful communication." How do you know when two people have successfully communicated?
- What inhibits clear communication? What promotes clear communication?
- In this activity, the two teams had to create identical "keys" to open a door. What "key" will help unlock the potential within your team? Who possesses this key?

Motivators

Clarity and understanding played a key role in this activity. In the quotes below, both of these issues are mentioned.

- What are the authors of these quotes saying to you?

"More important than the quest for certainty is the quest for clarity." - *Francois Gautier*

"Peace cannot be kept by force; it can only be achieved by understanding."
-*Albert Einstein (1879-1955), German physicist who developed the special and general theories of relativity; awarded the Nobel Prize for Physics in 1921*

"Everything that irritates us about others can lead us to an understanding of ourselves." - *Carl Jung (1875-1961), Swiss psychiatrist, psychologist and founder of Analytic Psychology*

95

ACTIVITY (15) .... NO LOOSE ENDS ....

Objectives

- Collaborate with team members to build a structure with no loose ends
- Work cooperatively as a team
- Listen to the ideas of others
- Show persistence in completing the activity
- Participate in a group conversation to process and evaluate the experience

Preparation

Time: 1 minute
Materials: 1 Toobeez set per group
chart paper (optional)
Setup:
1. Supply each group with one set of Toobeez.

Character Focus

Perseverance

Activity Plan

Group Size: 2 – 5

Time: 10 – 45 minutes

Mental Intensity: 2

Physical Intensity: 1

Space: Minimal

The Challenge

Create a structure with no dead ends.

96

No Loose Ends

Safety Reminders!

Appropriate caution is important to conduct these activities in a safe manner. Be sure to review these reminders prior to beginning the activity, and if necessary, share reminders with the group during the activity.

> • Follow general safety procedures

> • This is a real puzzle of an activity, and it can take some groups five minutes while others will struggle for 30 minutes

> See page 6 for available teambuilding training options!

Activity Instructions

1. Circle up the group, and share the following storyline.

> You are a team of scientists, and you must design the pipe system for the delivery of fresh air in an underwater research station. The air must be able to freely move and circulate. If the air hits a "dead end," it will no longer be useable.

97

No Loose Ends

2. Read aloud the following Activity Challenge Box to the group.

> **Challenge**: Create a structure with no dead ends. Follow the guidelines below:
> - There can be no "dead ends" in the structure
> - The Toobeez must be connected in the normal way. Do not bend or reconfigure the tubes or balls to force a fit to the point that the tube and/or ball is damaged
> - If any guidelines are broken, the group must begin again

3. To begin the activity, have participants first work through the Problem-Solving Sequence (refer to page 152 for the six sequence steps).

4. If participants get stuck, have the students circle up again. Use questions to help guide the group back on track, but do not provide the participants with answers. Allow them to work together.

5. If your group is still struggling OR if you feel your group would benefit from an additional challenge, present the variation provided on the next page.

6. After the activity, move to the "Activity Discussion and Processing" section of the activity.

98

Activity Variations

1. Build in three dimensions.
This activity is easier when you allow the group to build their structure in three dimensions. Requiring the group to build in only two dimensions (that is, flat on the floor) is more difficult.

Activity Notes

Acknowledgments
I first learned this activity from Jim Cain,
co-author of *Teamwork & Teamplay*.

Activity Discussion and Processing

Discussion Topic: Perseverance

In the storyline, you were asked to connect the Toobeez pieces in such a way that air could flow through the system without ever finding a "dead end." The air in the storyline represents a valuable resource that, if not allowed to circulate throughout the system, becomes unusable.

Discussion Questions

- What are the valuable resources on your team?
- Do we have systems which promote the circulation (sharing) of valuable resources? What effect does this have?
- In the storyline, you are asked to create a "closed system" so valuable air could not escape nor could new and valuable resources be added. What are the benefits of a closed system? What are the benefits of an open system? What kind of system do we have on this team?

Motivator

In the storyline, you were asked to create a system to circulate air. Below are quotes that mention the word "air."

- What are these quotes saying to you?

"Man can live about forty days without food, about three days without water, about eight minutes without air, but only for one second without hope." - *Anonymous*

"Our most basic common link is that we all inhabit this planet. We all breathe the same air. We all cherish our children's future. And we are all mortal."
- *John Fitzgerald Kennedy (1917-1963), 35ᵗʰ President of the United States*

ACTIVITY 16 ..... PHOTO FINISH .....

Objectives

- Cooperate with team members to cross the finish line at the same time
- Use communication to synchronize movements
- Work cooperatively toward a common goal
- Participate in a group conversation to process and evaluate the experience

Preparation

Time: 1 minute
Materials: 4 Toobeez tubes
chart paper (optional)

Setup:
1. Connect the four Toobeez end to end.
2. Place the finish line in the middle of the room.

Character Focus
Citizenship

Activity Plan

Group Size: 6 – 20

Time: 10 – 25 minutes

Mental Intensity: 2

Physical Intensity: 1

Space: Medium

The Challenge
The group must cross the Toobeez finish line at exactly the same time.

101

Photo Finish

Safety Reminders!

Appropriate caution is important to conduct these activities in a safe manner. Be sure to review these reminders prior to beginning the activity, and if necessary, share reminders with the group during the activity.

> • Follow general safety procedures

> • It is likely that someone in the group will inadvertently cross the plane of the finish line. Should this happen, the facilitator says, "Click!" This represents one of the group's five attempts. Hopefully the group will take greater care around the finish line
> • Use a digital camera to take a picture of each attempt to help validate a ruling

> See page 6 for available teambuilding training options!

Activity Instructions

1. Circle up the group, and share the following storyline.

> Normally, an Olympic race is about crossing the finish line before anyone else. In an effort to emphasize teamwork and unity, Olympic officials have designed a NEW type of race which requires participants to cross the finish line at precisely the same time. Now it is your turn. Show the world how your team can work as one!

102

Photo Finish

2. Read aloud the following Activity Challenge Box to the group.

> **Challenge**: The group must cross the Toobeez finish line at exactly the same time. Follow the guidelines below:
> - The group has 15 minutes to make five attempts to cross the finish line (break the vertical plane of the finish line) at exactly the same time
> - If any guidelines are broken, the group must begin again

3. To begin the activity, have participants first work through the Problem-Solving Sequence (refer to page 152 for the six sequence steps).
4. Gather the team on one side of the finish line and explain the rules.
5. The facilitator should be positioned at one end of the finish line to judge.
6. Each time someone breaks the plane of the finish line, the facilitator says, "Click!"
7. If participants get stuck, have the students circle up again. Use questions to help guide the group back on track, but do not provide the participants with answers. Allow them to work together.
8. If your group is still struggling OR if you feel your group would benefit from an additional challenge, present a variation provided on the next page.
9. After the activity, move to the "Activity Discussion and Processing" section of the activity.

Photo Finish

Activity Variations

1. Bring the finish line closer.

To make things MUCH harder, stand the team up with their backs against a wall and place the finish line only three feet in front of the group. This little twist makes planning much more difficult because they have minimal room.

2. Move the finish line further away.

To decrease the difficulty, setup the finish line in the middle of the room where a team has plenty of space to discuss and make a plan.

Activity Notes

Acknowledgments
Sam Sikes of doingworks.com is credited
with developing this game.

www.project-connect.net   www.TeachMeTeamwork.com

Photo Finish

Activity Discussion and Processing

Discussion Topic: Positive and persistent thinking

In this activity, participants were asked to work as one team to cross the finish line. Solving this challenge together as one requires an advanced form of thinking called "win-win" thinking. Thought processes and the actions taken fall into one of three categories:

1. Lose-Lose: You lose out and so does the other person; neither party wins.
2. Win-Lose: You win while the other person loses, or you lose while the other person wins.
3. Win-Win: You both win and get what you need. Win-Win thinking is "higher level" thinking.

What we typically see on the television, whether it is the evening news, a sports program or a cartoon, is either Lose-Lose or Win-Lose behavior. Getting a Win-Win behavior requires a "shift" in thinking.

Discussion Questions

- What lessons from competitive sports are useful for participating on a non-sports team (like in a classroom or for a business)?
- What lessons from competitive sports have no place on a non-sports team?
- Crossing the finish line as a team was most likely much more difficult for your group than if you would have been required to cross separately. What strategies did you use to work together that you would have not needed if working alone?

Motivator

In the storyline, you were asked to imagine your team as competitors in an Olympic race.

- Is the following message still useful or is it outdated?

"Nothing in this world can take the place of persistence. Talent will not; nothing is more common than unsuccessful people with talent. Genius will not; unrewarded genius is almost a proverb. Education will not; the world is full of educated derelicts. Persistence and determination alone are omnipotent. The slogan "Press on" has solved and always will solve the problems of the human race." - *Calvin Coolidge (1872-1933), 30th President of the United States*

105

ROBOT WRITER

Objectives

- Collaborate with team members to write a message using the "robot writer"
- Communicate with others to synchronize movements
- Work cooperatively toward a common goal
- Participate in a group conversation to process and evaluate the experience

Preparation

Time: 1 minute
Materials: 1 Toobeez set
　　　　　　tape
　　　　　　1 marker
　　　　　　1 large piece of paper
　　　　　　chart paper (optional)

Setup:
1. Build a "robot writer" (refer to photo). You may need masking tape to secure the marker.
2. Tape a piece of paper to the floor.

Character Focus
Cooperation

Activity Plan

Group Size: 2 – 8

Time: 5 – 15 minutes

Mental Intensity: 2

Physical Intensity: 1

Space: Minimal

The Challenge
The group must use the "robot writer" to write a word on a piece of paper.

Robot Writer

Safety Reminders!

Appropriate caution is important to conduct these activities in a safe manner. Be sure to review these reminders prior to beginning the activity, and if necessary, share reminders with the group during the activity.

> • Follow general safety procedures

> • Use a bigger piece of paper than you see in the photos. Bigger paper helps prevent the group from writing on the floor
> • Use water-based markers (non-permanent ink markers)

Activity Instructions

1. Circle up the group, and share the following storyline.

> You are a team of genetic engineers working to discover a new way to produce rice to help end world hunger. The rice must be easy to grow, insect resistant, organic (grown without pesticides), nutritious and totally healthy. To work on this new rice seed, you must operate mechanical arms while deciphering the genetic code of this new "super food" (to the average person it will look like you are writing words). By working together smoothly and efficiently, you will be able to end world hunger.

107

Robot Writer

2. Read aloud the following Activity Challenge Box to the group.

> **Challenge**: The group must use the "robot writer" to write a word on a piece of paper. Follow the guidelines below:
> - The robot must be held by the ball at the end of the tube
> - The robot writer may not be altered
> - If any guidelines are broken, the group must begin again

3. To begin the activity, have participants first work through the Problem-Solving Sequence (refer to page 152 for the six sequence steps).

4. Have the group create something with their "robot writer." They can: A) write the word TEAM, B) draw a smiley face, C) draw a figure eight, or D) anything else!

5. If participants get stuck, have the students circle up again. Use questions to help guide the group back on track, but do not provide the participants with answers. Allow them to work together.

6. If your group is still struggling OR if you feel your group would benefit from an additional challenge, present a variation provided on the next page.

7. After the activity, move to the "Activity Discussion and Processing" section of the activity.

> See page 6 for available teambuilding training options!

Robot Writer

Activity Variations

1. Increasing the difficulty.
To make this activity more challenging, create a robot writer with long arms, do not allow verbal communication or require use of the non-dominant hand.

2. Follow the maze.
Create a maze on a piece of paper (like the kind in children's books). Have the group make the robot writer marker follow the correct pathway through the maze.

3. Make geometry.
Draw different shapes as a team, such as triangles, squares or a figure 8.

4. The leader.
Everyone on the team closes their eyes except one. This person is allowed to keep their eyes open for one minute and will direct the team. At the end of one minute, they close their eyes and someone else on the team opens their eyes for one minute. Rotate this responsibility so everyone has a turn to direct the team.

5. A real challenge.
When working with a more sophisticated group, ask them to draw out the school logo. Provide them with all the colored markers they need. This logo becomes their "deliverable" and you become the customer. Provide them with a short time frame to accomplish everything. At the end of this time frame, they must deliver a presentation

Activity Notes

Acknowledgments
I first learned this activity from Jim Cain, co-author of *Teamwork & Teamplay*.

www.project-connect.net   www.TeachMeTeamwork.com

Robot Writer

Activity Discussion and Processing

Discussion Topic: Teamwork/Cooperation
In the storyline, the participants are a group of scientists working to create a food source to end world hunger. This is an excellent activity to talk about the world of science and the role teamwork plays in it.

Discussion Questions
- Individuals working alone can often solve small challenges. However, large challenges are usually solved by groups of people working together. Explain why this is true
- When a team finds a solution to a problem, who should take the credit? Should it be the leader of the team?
- To successfully solve this challenge, your team had to work in harmony. The word "harmony" is usually used when talking about or describing music. How is a team that works well together like beautiful music?

Motivator
In the storyline, the team was asked to work on deciphering a "genetic code." The word "genetic" is mentioned in the following quotes.
- What are these people saying?
- What do their quotes have to do with your team?

"The most dangerous leadership myth is that leaders are born - that there is a genetic factor to leadership. This myth asserts that people simply either have certain charismatic qualities or not. That's nonsense; in fact, the opposite is true. Leaders are made rather than born." - *Warren G. Bennis*

"The one process now going on that will take millions of years to correct is the loss of genetic and species diversity by the destruction of natural habitats. This is the folly our descendants are least likely to forgive us." - *Edward O. Wilson*

110

ACTIVITY (18)

SIDES SWITCH

Objectives

- Collaborate to switch places with other team members
- Communicate and cooperate with team members
- Show awareness of other team members
- Participate in a group conversation to process and evaluate the experience

Preparation

Time: 4 minutes

Materials: 1 Toobeez set
chart paper (optional)

Setup:

1. Build a long rectangle (refer to photo) with blue squares on one side and red squares on the other. The more narrow the rectangle, the more difficult the activity. In the photo shown, the width of the rectangle is set by the shortest tube.

Character Focus
Respecting Others

Activity Plan
Group Size: 4 – 12
Time: 5 – 25 minutes
Mental Intensity: 1
Physical Intensity: 3
Space: Medium

The Challenge
The people on the blue side must switch places with the people on the red side.

111

Sides Switch

Safety Reminders!

Appropriate caution is important to conduct these activities in a safe manner. Be sure to review these reminders prior to beginning the activity, and if necessary, share reminders with the group during the activity.

- Follow general safety procedures
- People may lose their balance in this activity. Remind people to step out of the rectangle if they lose their balance (rather than fall out)

- Changing places requires a great deal of physical contact on the part of the participants. For this reason, make sure your group is ready to work in close proximity. This may not be an appropriate activity for mixed groups of male and female
- This activity is simple if only four people are participating. The more people you add, the harder this activity gets
- It is nice to have an even number of players

Activity Instructions

1. Circle up the group, and share the following storyline.

> Your team is on a television "reality" show where you are presented with challenges in the wilderness. This new challenge has your team standing on a narrow log suspended above a raging icy-cold river. Team members on either side of the log must switch places. If you fall off (if you step outside the Toobeez squares), you will be swept down the river into a rescue net. Complete this challenge and your team will advance to the next challenge.

112

Sides Switch

2. Read aloud the following Activity Challenge Box to the group.

> **Challenge**: The people on the blue side must switch places with the people on the red side. Follow the guidelines below:
> - Participants may not stand on the rectangle
> - Participants may not touch the ground outside the rectangle
> - The Toobeez structure may not be altered
> - If any guidelines are broken, the group must begin again

3. To begin the activity, have participants first work through the Problem-Solving Sequence (refer to page 152 for the six sequence steps).

4. Have the team stand inside the rectangle. Ask four people to stand in a row, one behind the other. Then ask the other four people to stand one behind the other facing the other group. Tell each group that they must switch places with the other group. For example: Start = **1 2 3 4 5 6 7 8**, End = **5 6 7 8 1 2 3 4** (where the numbers are the people; refer to the picture).

5. If participants get stuck, have the students circle up again. Use questions to help guide the group back on track, but do not provide the participants with answers. Allow them to work together.

6. If your group is still struggling OR if you feel your group would benefit from an additional challenge, present a variation provided on the next page.

7. After the activity, move to the "Activity Discussion and Processing" section of the activity.

113

Sides Switch

Activity Variations

1. Changing the level of difficulty.

Change the width of the rectangle to vary the difficulty: the more narrow the rectangle, the harder the activity.

2. Mix up the order.

Ask the group to stand inside the rectangle. Then ask them to arrange themselves by birth date, height or the first letter of their last name.

3. Increase the difficulty.

Make a giant plus sign by placing a rectangle perpendicular to the rectangle already created. You will have four smaller groups switching places all at the same time. This is hard.

See page 6 for available teambuilding training options!

Activity Notes

Acknowledgments

Karl Rohnke provided a description of this activity in his book, *Silver Bullets*, published in 1984.

Activity Discussion and Processing

Discussion Topic: Respecting and Helping Others

This activity requires people to support each other as they switch places. It also forces people to work in close proximity to each other. These two requirements create a backdrop for the debrief session.

Discussion Questions

- As you moved from your original position to your final position, what did you notice about how people helped each other? Which of these helpful behaviors would you like to see repeated on a regular basis with your team?
- Describe the behaviors that will be the easiest to repeat and which will be the hardest to repeat
- While you were waiting for your turn to move to your final position, what was the most helpful thing you did for the team?
- Who is there to support you in real life? Is it important to develop a "support network?"

Motivator

To complete this activity successfully, team members needed to cooperate, maintain balance and be patient. In the following quotes, each of these important life skills is mentioned.

- What are these people saying, and how is it important to your team?

"Power consists in one's capacity to link his will with the purpose of others, to lead by reason and a gift of **cooperation**." - *Woodrow T. Wilson (1856-1924), 28th President of the United States*

"Life is like riding a bicycle. To keep your **balance** you must keep moving."
- *Albert Einstein (1879-1955), German physicist who developed the special and general theories of relativity; awarded the Nobel Prize for Physics in 1921*

"Every great dream begins with a dreamer. Always remember, you have within you the strength, the **patience**, and the passion to reach for the stars to change the world." - *Harriet Tubman (1820-1913), American escaped slave, Civil War soldier and abolitionist*

115

ACTIVITY 19 ..... SNAKE .....

Objectives

- Collaborate with team members to pass the rope through the tower
- Use communication and cooperation skills to work as a team
- Participate in a group conversation to process and evaluate the experience

Preparation

Time: 5 minutes
Materials: 1 Toobeez set
100 feet of rope
chart paper (optional)

Setup:
1. Build a tower using Toobeez (refer to photo). The more holes you build into the tower, the harder the activity will be.

Character Focus

Responsibility & Teamwork

Activity Plan

Group Size: 8 – 16

Time: 10 – 20 minutes

Mental Intensity: 2

Physical Intensity: 1

Space: Minimal

The Challenge

The group must pass a piece of rope through every hole in the tower.

Snake

Safety Reminders!

Appropriate caution is important to conduct these activities in a safe manner. Be sure to review these reminders prior to beginning the activity, and if necessary, share reminders with the group during the activity.

- Follow general safety procedures

- This activity is similar to Activity #7: Cube and Activity #21: Spider's Web found in this guide. The difference is the group is not passing a person, so it is much safer
- This activity requires the group to focus and can be a good lead-in activity to the Cube and the Spider's Web activities

See page 6 for available teambuilding training options!

Activity Instructions

1. Circle up the group, and share the following storyline.

> The authorities have discovered a dangerous situation. A power grid (a small tower) in the city's electrical system must be deactivated before it causes the entire system to shut down. To deactivate the grid, a long wire must pass through each of the tower's openings. It is tricky business. If the wire rope touches the tower, the entire electrical grid for the city will shut down, causing a catastrophe. Your team has been called in to solve the problem.

Project Connect: Toobeez Teambuilding Activity Workbook

Snake

2. Read aloud the following Activity Challenge Box to the group.

> **Challenge**: The group must pass a piece of rope through every hole in the tower. Follow the guidelines below:
> - The rope must be passed through ALL "openings" in the tower. An opening is defined as any complete geometric shape (square, rectangle, etc.) made from the Toobeez
> - Clumping, folding, cutting or other efforts to make the rope shorter are not allowed
> - The Toobeez tower may not be touched by anything
> - The tower may not be moved or altered
> - Team members must keep at least one foot on the ground at all times
> - If any guidelines are broken, the group must begin again

3. To begin the activity, have participants first work through the Problem-Solving Sequence (refer to page 152 for the six sequence steps).
4. The group can then begin to move the rope through the openings in a snake-like fashion.
5. If participants get stuck, have the students circle up again. Use questions to help guide the group back on track, but do not provide the participants with answers. Allow them to work together.
6. If your group is still struggling OR if you feel your group would benefit from an additional challenge, present the variation provided on the next page.
7. After the activity, move to the "Activity Discussion and Processing" section of the activity.

Snake

Activity Variations

1. Use a shorter rope.
In the photos, you see a group passing 100 feet of rope through the tower. To make the task easier, provide a shorter rope (for example, 50 feet). The longer rope requires the group to focus for a longer period of time.

Activity Notes

Acknowledgments
Mike Anderson of Learning Works, Inc. is credited with creating this game.

Snake

Activity Discussion and Processing

Discussion Topic: Commitment

I like to use this activity to bring up issues around commitment to a task or goal. When the rope is long (100+ feet), it is easy for the group to get lackadaisical because it can take so long to pass the rope through the holes. Sometimes a team will know how to do something, but they lack the willpower to see it through. The people who are the most successful (the best of the best) have amazing willpower.

Discussion Questions

- What is your personal willpower on a scale of 1 to 10 (with 1 being low and 10 being high)?
- What is your personal willpower when you are tired and/or hungry?
- How would you rate your team's willpower on a scale of 1 to 10? What would you like it to be? Why?

Motivator

In this activity, patience and commitment to the goal played a big role. In the quotes below, both authors speak of commitment and fortitude.

- What do these quotes say to you?

"Patience and fortitude conquer all things." - *Ralph Waldo Emerson (1803-1882), American poet, lecturer and essayist*

"Until one is committed, there is hesitancy, the chance to draw back, always ineffectiveness. Concerning all acts of initiative and creation, there is one elementary truth - the ignorance of which kills countless ideas and splendid plans: that the moment one definitely commits oneself, then providence moves too. All sorts of things occur to help one that would never otherwise have occurred. A whole stream of events issues from the decision, raising in one's favor all manner of unforeseen incidents, meetings and material assistance which no man could have dreamed would have come his way. Whatever you can do or dream you can, begin it. Boldness has genius, power and magic in it. Begin it now." – *Johann Wolfgang von Goethe (1749-1832), German playwright, poet, novelist and dramatist*

ACTIVITY 20 .... SOLO HIGH JUMP ....

Objectives

- Develop strategies to jump over the tube
- Show persistence to complete the activity
- Rely on self to be successful
- Participate in a group conversation to process and evaluate the experience

Preparation

Time: None
Materials: 1 long Toobeez per person
chart paper (optional)
Setup:
1. Provide each person with a long Toobeez tube.

Character Focus
Uniqueness

Activity Plan

Group Size: 1 at a time

Time: 5 – 10 minutes

Mental Intensity: 1

Physical Intensity: 3

Space: Minimal

The Challenge
Each participant will jump over the tube.

121

Solo High Jump

Safety Reminders!

Appropriate caution is important to conduct these activities in a safe manner. Be sure to review these reminders prior to beginning the activity, and if necessary, share reminders with the group during the activity.

- Follow general safety procedures
- This activity is dangerous no matter how you look at it. The person jumping can easily hurt themselves in a number of ways
- Out of each group of ten average people, there is usually one who can successfully jump the tube. The others who are watching this one successful person might be tempted to jump even though, deep down, they know they should not

 **Helpful Hints!**

- Do not offer this activity if you are concerned about someone getting hurt
- Even though it is dangerous and tricky to do, this is a fun activity with a lot to offer in terms of debriefing

Activity Instructions

1. Circle up the group, and share the following storyline.

> While traveling in a far and distant land, you encounter a small village populated by people with a strange custom. It seems they like to do a "solo high jump" which, to them, demonstrates a commitment to self-improvement and moving beyond self-imposed limitations. As the honored guest at an evening meal with the mayor of the village, you are expected to "solo high jump." Show them what you have got!

2. Read aloud the following Activity Challenge Box to the group.

Challenge: Each participant will jump over the tube. Follow the guideline below:

- During the jump, the jumper must hold onto the tube with both hands at all times

---

3. To begin the activity, have participants first work through the Problem-Solving Sequence (refer to page 152 for the six sequence steps).

4. For the forward jump, the jumper stands holding the tube in their hands in a horizontal fashion. The tube starts out in front of them and will end up behind them.

5. Be sure to monitor each participant for safety as he or she attempts the activity.

6. If participants get stuck, have the students circle up again. Use questions to help guide the group back on track, but do not provide the participants with answers. Allow them to work together.

7. If your group is still struggling OR if you feel your group would benefit from an additional challenge, present a variation provided on the next page.

8. After the activity, move to the "Activity Discussion and Processing" section of the activity.

Solo High Jump

Activity Variations

1. Jump backward.
Start with the tube behind you and end up with the tube in front of you.
2. Close your eyes.
If you really want to test coordination, have participants jump forward with their eyes closed. Save yourself some time, and dial 911 before you attempt this.

Activity Notes

See page 6 for available teambuilding training options!

Acknowledgments
I was taught this activity by a camper in a YMCA program.

Solo High Jump

Activity Discussion and Processing

Discussion Topic: Overcoming personal obstacles

Most people encounter obstacles (hurdles) as they pursue their dreams and aspirations. These obstacles might be small, large, repeat often or occur infrequently. Regardless of the type of obstacle one faces, it is useful to 1) be able to identify an obstacle, 2) be able to identify the best way to deal with an obstacle, and 3) if the situation demands it, be able to fully commit to move through the obstacle.

Discussion Questions

- Describe an obstacle with which you have had to deal. What did you learn from having to deal with this obstacle?
- Describe the top three obstacles your team faced. How did working through these obstacles cause your team to grow in a positive way?
- Have you ever decided on a goal that seemed impossible or highly risky? What did you learn from it?

Motivator

The following two quotes mention the word "jump." One talks of jumping over hurdles and the other of jumping a distance greater than what is currently thought possible.

- How are these messages similar?
- What do these quotes say to you?

"You have to find something that you love enough to be able to take risks, **jump** over the hurdles and break through the brick walls that are always going to be placed in front of you. If you don't have that kind of feeling for what it is you are doing, you'll stop at the first giant hurdle." - *George Lucas, American film director and producer; famous for his epic* Star Wars *and* Indiana Jones *trilogies*

"Scientists have proven that it's impossible to long-**jump** 30 feet, but I don't listen to that kind of talk. Thoughts like that have a way of sinking into your feet."
- *Carl Lewis, Olympic long-jump record holder*

125

ACTIVITY 21 ..... SPIDER'S WEB ....

Objectives

- Collaborate with team members to move through the web in unique ways
- Communicate with the group to complete the activity
- Rely on group members
- Participate in a group conversation to process and evaluate the experience

Preparation

Time: 5 minutes
Materials: 1 Toobeez set
                        chart paper (optional)
Setup:
1. Build a rectangular-shaped tower using Toobeez (refer to photo). The tower should be approximatley 6' high. The more narrow the tower, the harder the activity.

Character Focus
Trust & Caring

Activity Plan
Group Size: 10 – 15
Time: 25 – 45 minutes
Mental Intensity: 2
Physical Intensity: 3
Space: Medium

The Challenge
Pass your entire team through the spider's web before time runs out.

126

Spider's Web

Safety Reminders!

Appropriate caution is important to conduct these activities in a safe manner. Be sure to review these reminders prior to beginning the activity, and if necessary, share reminders with the group during the activity.

- Proper spotting techniques must be reviewed prior to starting this challenge (refer to the "Safety Procedures" section on page 19)
- It is ideal to have cushions or pads placed under the Toobeez structure to minimize the effects of a fall
- All participants must be spotted as they travel through the cube
- If your group is not physically strong enough, mature enough and/or calm enough, do not attempt this activity

- A tower with high openings is more challenging
- Rather than building the spider's web for the group, have them build it
- Some groups may want to practice passing people through the spider's web prior to actually starting. **Note:** Allowing the group to practice on the web itself can take away some of the unknown aspects of the activity. Consider setting limitations on the practice (time, number of tries, etc.)

Activity Instructions

1. Circle up the group, and share the following storyline.

> While on a caving expedition, your team encounters a strange three-dimensional spider's web blocking the tunnel your team must follow. You have heard stories of a giant spider that lives in the cave, and you do not want to find out if the stories are true. Get your team through the spider's web, but do not touch it otherwise the spider might show up.

127

Spider's Web

2. Read aloud the following Activity Challenge Box to the group.

Challenge: Pass your entire team through the spider's web before time runs out. Follow the guidelines below:

- Each team member must pass through the spider's web using a unique pathway. Once a pathway is used, that unique sequence of travel cannot be used again
- The spider's web must not be touched by anything
- Participants may not jump or dive through openings
- Team members may not be launched through the openings
- Anyone traveling through the spider's web must be spotted
- No other equipment may be used in this activity
- The group *MUST* complete this activity in a safe manner or the activity will be stopped
- If any guidelines are broken, the group may be given a penalty (see Step #6)

---

3. To begin the activity, have participants first work through the Problem-Solving Sequence (refer to page 152 for the six sequence steps).
4. Teach or review proper spotting techniques (refer to the "Safety Procedures" section on page 19).
5. Be sure to monitor the group for safety as they attempt the activity.
6. If a touch occurs, choose one of the following penalties: A) everyone starts again, B) only one person has to travel back through the web, C) the group may not communicate verbally for five minutes, or D) a combination of these.

128

Spider's Web

7. If participants get stuck, have the students circle up again. Use questions to help guide the group back on track, but do not provide the participants with answers. Allow them to work together.

8. If your group is still struggling OR if you feel your group would benefit from an additional challenge, present the variation provided below.

9. After the activity, move to the "Activity Discussion and Processing" section of the activity.

> See page 6 for available teambuilding training options!

Activity Variations

1. **Providing opportunity for new group leadership.**

There is a tendency for one or two people to be the most vocal. Have them suddenly become mute so that they can still participate, but can not speak.

Activity Notes

> ### Acknowledgments
> Karl Rohnke provided a description of this activity in his book, *Silver Bullets,* published in 1984.

Spider's Web

Activity Discussion and Processing

Discussion Topic: Overcoming obstacles
In nature, spider webs represent one of the most familiar ways to passively catch prey. The spider spins its web and then waits for its prey to get caught. Unlike the unknowing fly, people (or teams) can, if they so choose, become aware of obstacles in their path and choose to go through them – or not.

Discussion Questions
- Are there obstacles in your (or your team's) path that you can avoid?
- Are there obstacles which you must face? If yes, what did you practice in this activity that will help your team successfully overcome these obstacles?
- Who was lifted through the spider's web? Describe what it felt like to be lifted through

Motivator
In the storyline, your team must travel through a spider's web. Each of the following quotes mentions a web, though each uses the metaphor of the web in a different way.
- What are these people saying, and what do you think they mean?
- Can you apply their message to your own situation (on this team or in life)?

"When spider webs unite, they can tie up a lion." - *Ethiopian proverb*

"Any act often repeated soon forms a habit; and habit allowed, steady gains in strength. At first it may be but as a spider's web, easily broken through, but if not resisted it soon binds us with chains of steel." - *Tryon Edwards (1809-1894)*

"We live in a web of ideas, a fabric of our own making." - *Joseph Chilton Pearce*

ACTIVITY 22 ..... TALLEST TOWER ....

Objectives

- Collaborate with team members to build the tallest tower
- Work cooperatively as a team
- Communicate and listen to the ideas of others
- Participate in a group conversation to process and evaluate the experience

Preparation

Time: 1 minute

Materials: 1 Toobeez set
chart paper (optional)

Setup:

1. Divide the contents of the Toobeez set between the two teams. If you have only one team, you may provide them with an entire set of Toobeez, but please read the safety reminders regaring this choice.

Character Focus
Communication

Activity Plan

Group Size: 2 – 5

Time: 10 – 25 minutes

Mental Intensity: 2

Physical Intensity: 1

Space: Medium

The Challenge

Working as a team, build the tallest tower that you can.

Tallest Tower

Safety Reminders!

Appropriate caution is important to conduct these activities in a safe manner. Be sure to review these reminders prior to beginning the activity, and if necessary, share reminders with the group during the activity.

- Follow general safety procedures
- Towers may fall over. Be careful not to get hit by a falling tower
- You can supply a team with an entire set of Toobeez (52 pieces), but watch out! The tower they build will be very tall and potentially very dangerous if it falls over

- Keep the size of each team small (two to five people). When the teams are larger, people end up standing around watching rather than participating
- You will note that one guideline states everyone must keep at least one foot on the ground. This is to prevent people from sitting (or standing) on teammates' shoulders as they build a tall tower. It also prevents people from standing on chairs, tables, ladders, etc. What people will learn to do is build the tower horizontally and then erect it vertically

Activity Instructions

1. Circle up the group, and share the following storyline.

> Your team is stranded on a distant island. The radio you have is working, but you need a tall antenna to get the signal out so the search and rescue team can find you. Build the tallest freestanding radio tower you can so your radio signal will be heard and you will get rescued.

132

Tallest Tower

2. Read aloud the following Activity Challenge Box to the group.

> **Challenge**: Working as a team, build the tallest tower that you can. Follow the guidelines below:
> - Each tower must be free-standing and must be able to support itself for 30 seconds
> - The height of the tower will be measured from the floor
> - Only Toobeez can be used to build the tower
> - All team members must keep at least one foot on the floor at all times
> - Team members may not interfere with another team's tower
> - If any guidelines are broken, the group must begin again

3. To begin the activity, have participants first work through the Problem-Solving Sequence (refer to page 152 for the six sequence steps).

4. If you set up this activity to be competitive (that is, two or more teams building towers), you will have opportunities to discuss how the team members handled competition. Some people will do anything and say anything just to win – even at the expense of the relationships with their own teammates. If you see this type of behavior, address it. Ask them if their behavior creates a culture of sustainability and excellence (you may first have to define these terms with the group).

5. If participants get stuck, have the students circle up again. Use questions to help guide the group back on track, but do not provide the participants with answers. Allow them to work together.

6. If your group is still struggling OR if you feel your group would benefit from an additional challenge, present the variation provided on the next page.

7. After the activity, move to the "Activity Discussion and Processing" section of the activity.

> See page 6 for available teambuilding training options!

133

Tallest Tower

Activity Variations

1. Cooperative play without competition.
Consider creating a situation where the small teams work together. For example, challenge the teams to build the tallest tower they can. When the towers are complete, measure each tower and add the measurements of each tower together to create a TOTAL TOWER MEASUREMENT. Then, ask the groups to disassemble their towers and build new towers using the best practices they discovered from all the teams. The goal is to build towers that are taller than before, beating the TOTAL TOWER height of the first round. This way, all teams contribute to a win.

Activity Notes

Acknowledgments
Jim Cain, co-author of *Teamwork & Teamplay*,
first introduced this activity to me.

www.project-connect.net   www.TeachMeTeamwork.com

Tallest Tower

Activity Discussion and Processing

Discussion Topic: Communication

If you set up this activity to be competitive, you will have opportunities to discuss how the team members dealt with their own competitive nature. Some people will do anything and say anything just to win - even at the expense of the relationships with their own teammates.

Discussion Questions

- (If you observe hyper-competitive behavior, ask the following) What do "excellence" and "sustainability" mean? Do your behavior choices around competition create a culture of sustainability and excellence on the team? In the community at large?
- If you were to build a real radio station tower, what message would you broadcast to the world? What message would improve the world?
- What message does your team "broadcast" on a daily basis?
- How do you know when communication has occurred? How do you know when someone really understands what you have to say?
- Are you a better listener or a better talker?
- What can we do now that will improve our level of communication?
- What would happen on our team if we communicated more effectively?

Motivator

In the storyline, the team builds a tower to send out a message to save themselves.
- What about these quotes speaks to you or your team?

"I respect the man who knows distinctly what he wishes. The greater part of all mischief in the world arises from the fact that men do not sufficiently understand their own aims. They have undertaken to build a **tower**, and spend no more labor on the foundation than would be necessary to erect a hut." - *Johann Wolfgang von Goethe (1749-1832), German playwright, poet, novelist and dramatist*

"The most important thing in **communication** is to hear what isn't being said."
- *Peter F. Drucker, American educator and writer*

ACTIVITY 23 ...... TOUCH THE BALL ....

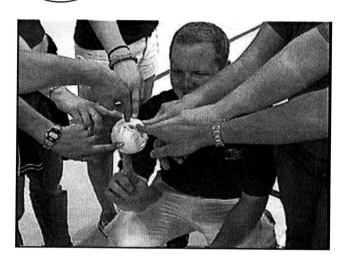

Objectives

- Cooperate with team members to touch the ball simultaneously
- Communicate with the team to synchronize movements
- Show awareness of others in the group
- Participate in a group conversation to process and evaluate the experience

Character Focus
Respecting Others

Preparation

Time: None
Materials: 1 Toobeez ball
             chart paper (optional)
Setup:
1. Select a Toobeez ball for the group to use.

Activity Plan

Group Size: 10 – 20

Time: 3 – 10 minutes

Mental Intensity: 1

Physical Intensity: 1

Space: Minimal

The Challenge
As a group, everyone must touch the ball at the same time.

136

Touch the Ball

Safety Reminders!

Appropriate caution is important to conduct these activities in a safe manner. Be sure to review these reminders prior to beginning the activity, and if necessary, share reminders with the group during the activity.

- Follow general safety procedures

- This is a great introductory level group problem-solving activity to do at the beginning of a program
- This activity requires people to be close physically, yet prohibits touching
- This is a great activity to lead with large groups (200+)

See page 6 for available teambuilding training options!

Activity Instructions

1. Circle up the group, and share the following storyline.

> While traveling through a mystical land, your team has come upon a magic door guarded by a wise old man. The guard tells you the door opens to a magical room where you can create any kind of world you can imagine. When you try turning the doorknob, you find the door is locked. The guard tells you the only way to open the door is if everyone on your team touches the yellow doorknob simultaneously without touching each other. Can your team open the door?

Touch the Ball

2. Read aloud the following Activity Challenge Box to the group.

> **Challenge**: As a group, everyone must touch the ball at the same time. Follow the guidelines below:
> - No touching anyone or anything else (includes hair and clothing)
> - Find a way for everyone to touch the ball at the same time
> - If any guidelines are broken, the group must begin again

3. To begin the activity, have participants first work through the Problem-Solving Sequence (refer to page 152 for the six sequence steps).
4. If participants get stuck, have the students circle up again. Use questions to help guide the group back on track, but do not provide the participants with answers. Allow them to work together.
5. If your group is still struggling OR if you feel your group would benefit from an additional challenge, present a variation provided on the next page.
6. After the activity, move to the "Activity Discussion and Processing" section of the activity.

Activity Variations

1. Increase the challenge.

After completing the basic challenge outlined above, add these rules: One person in the group must touch the ball with their nose, another with their elbow, another with their knee, and another with the tip of their shoe (which must stay on their foot). Give the group two minutes to solve this.

2. Leading with a large group.

Start off by supplying the group with lots of balls (about one ball per eight people). Tell the group that everyone must be touching a ball at the end of 30 seconds without touching anything else. Once everyone has succeeded (this is easy with a lot of balls), tell the group there has been a "reduction in funding" and they will have to do the same with less. This gives you the reason to take a couple of the balls. Now give the group 30 seconds to find a spot and touch a ball. Once they succeed, remove a few more balls and repeat this process.

Activity Notes

Acknowledgments

Karl Rohnke provided a description of this activity in his book, *Silver Bullets,* published in 1984.

Activity Discussion and Processing

Discussion Topic: Group potential

Oftentimes in education we seek to find the "key" that will unlock the door to an individual's potential. In this activity, we are presenting an opportunity to find a way to unlock the potential of the group.

Discussion Questions

- In the storyline, you are offered the opportunity to unlock the door to a magical kingdom where you can create a world based on your imagination. What would one find in a world you create? Who would be there? What types of rules (if any) would you have? How would it be different than our current world? In what ways would it be similar?

- To accomplish this challenge, your team placed a great deal of attention on the ball. What are the benefits of placing most or all of your attention on one task? What are the negatives? Where would you have your team place more focus/attention? What would the benefits be?

Motivator

Many a great teacher has talked about "opening doors." The following people talk about doors, and each one has a similar message.

- What are these great teachers telling you?

"Teachers open the **door**, but you must enter by yourself." - *Chinese proverb*

"Sometimes we stare so long at a **door** that is closing that we see too late the one that is open." - *Alexander Graham Bell (1847-1922), Scottish-born inventor and educator; best known for the invention of the telephone in 1876*

"When you follow your bliss... **doors** will open where you would not have thought there would be **doors**; and where there wouldn't be a **door** for anyone else."
- *Joseph Campbell (1904-1987), American author, editor, philosopher and teacher*

ACTIVITY 24 · · · · · · TOXIC GAS LEAK · · · · · ·

Preparation

Time: 5 minutes
Materials: 1 Toobeez set
40 feet of rope
chart paper (optional)

Setup:
1. Create a circular boundary using the rope.
2. Create two piles of Toobeez, with each pile containing the exact same pieces (colors do not have to match). Place one pile inside the roped-off area and the other pile outside the roped-off area.
3. Outside the roped-off area, create a structure (for example, a cube) using all or some of the pieces. This structure, "Structure A," will be the structure the group will duplicate.

Objectives

- Collaborate with team members to duplicate a structure
- Communicate with the group to complete the activity
- Rely on group members
- Participate in a group conversation to process and evaluate the experience

Character Focus
Communication

Activity Plan
Group Size: 5 – 20

Time: 15 – 45 minutes

Mental Intensity: 2

Physical Intensity: 3

Space: Medium

The Challenge
Use the Toobeez pieces inside the roped area to duplicate the Toobeez structure outside the roped area.

141

Toxic Gas Leak

Safety Reminders!

Appropriate caution is important to conduct these activities in a safe manner. Be sure to review these reminders prior to beginning the activity, and if necessary, share reminders with the group during the activity.

- Some people can get carried away with holding their breath, and they may get close to passing out. Remind people not to stay in the roped-off area too long (that is, do not hold your breath too long!)
- Follow general safety procedures

- The more complicated Structure A, the more difficult the challenge
- This activity is more difficult than it appears. It may be helpful to allow the group to cycle through all the team members and then provide them with one additional trip
- Allowing the group the opportunity to design the structure they must duplicate can be very empowering. This offers windows of opportunity to discuss topics such as "how to select the level of challenge that promotes the greatest growth"

Activity Instructions

1. Circle up the group, and share the following storyline.

    A freight train has derailed in your community, and your team has been called in to help with the cleanup. The train conductor tells you that one of the cars contains a highly concentrated form of laughing gas and that the pipes were damaged in the accident. A temporary "curtain" surrounds the car now, but that curtain will not contain the gas for long. If the gas leaks out, people all over the region will be laughing hysterically. The only way to permanently contain the gas is to repair the pipes. The gas container manufacturer has supplied a duplicate of the pipe structure. Your team must repair the gas container by duplicating the supplied pipe structure.

142

Toxic Gas Leak

2. Read aloud the following Activity Challenge Box to the group.

Challenge: Use the Toobeez pieces inside the roped area to duplicate the Toobeez structure outside the roped area. Follow the guidelines below:

- Participants may only use the Toobeez inside the roped area
- The finished structure must be an exact duplicate of Structure A in its shape (colors do not have to match)
- Each person is allowed one trip into the roped area
- When inside the roped area, you must keep your <u>eyes closed</u>
- No one on the outside may reach inside the roped area
- Team members can only stay inside the roped area for as long as they can hold their breath
- The boundary rope may not be moved
- If any guidelines are broken, the group must begin again

---

3. To begin the activity, have participants first work through the Problem-Solving Sequence (refer to page 152 for the six sequence steps).
4. The team has 20 minutes for this task, and the facilitator will track the time.
5. If participants get stuck, have the students circle up again. Use questions to help guide the group back on track, but do not provide the participants with answers. Allow them to work together.
6. If your group is still struggling OR if you feel your group would benefit from an additional challenge, present a variation provided on the next page.
7. After the activity, move to the "Activity Discussion and Processing" section of the activity.

143

Toxic Gas Leak

Activity Variations

1. Keeping your eyes open.
For younger age groups, you may want to allow them to keep their eyes open when they travel inside the roped off area (while keeping the breath-holding rule).

2. Add a stopwatch.
Replace the "hold your breath" rule with a stopwatch. Participants may only stay inside the roped-off area for a maximum of 30 seconds.

Activity Notes

See page 6 for available teambuilding training options!

Acknowledgments
I developed this activity for a business group.

144

Toxic Gas Leak

Activity Discussion and Processing

Discussion Topic: When to take action

One way this activity challenges a group is through the rule of "only one trip inside the rope boundary." What tends to happen is the people with little patience quickly take their turn without much planning (later reporting that they "wasted their turn"). On the other end of the spectrum, there is the person who waits and plans and waits and plans, and then runs out of time without ever taking a turn inside. If this pattern occurs (and it happens often), ask the group to explain the yin/yang balance of "think and do."

- In this activity, it seems to be easy for many team members to "sit and watch" and become a spectator to others who are fully engaged. Videotape a group doing this activity and play it back to them to discuss this phenomenon

Discussion Questions

- When is it time to take action? When is it time to think and plan? Does your team have a balance of "think" and "do" personalities?
- What are the benefits of sitting and watching? What are the benefits and challenges of choosing full engagement (in this activity and in life)?

Motivator

In this activity, you are working to stop a leak. In the following quotes, the authors also mention leaks, but in different ways.

- How do the following two people view leaks?
- Which quote relates more to you?

"Beware of little expenses; a small leak can sink a great ship." - *Benjamin Franklin (1706-1790), American statesman, scientist, philosopher, printer, writer and inventor*

"Lie down and listen to the crabgrass grow, the faucet leak, and learn to leave them so." - *Marya Mannes (1904-1990), American writer*

145

JOIN TOGETHER

No pictures are available at this time for this activity.

Objectives

- Work as a team to connect the entire group
- Participate in a group conversation to process and evaluate the experience

Preparation

Time: 1 minute
Materials: 1 Toobeez set
chart paper (optional)
Setup:
1. Hand out one piece of Toobeez to each person (either a tube or a ball).

Character Focus

Teamwork

The Challenge

The entire group must connect.

See page 6 for available teambuilding training options!

Activity Plan

Group Size: 30 – 52

Time: 2 – 5 minutes

Mental Intensity: 1

Physical Intensity: 1

Space: Lots

146

Bonus: Join Together

Safety Reminders!

Appropriate caution is important to conduct these activities in a safe manner. Be sure to review these reminders prior to beginning the activity, and if necessary, share reminders with the group during the activity.

- Follow general safety procedures

 *Helpful Hints!*

- This is an activity for a large group. It works best when you have between 40 and 52 people (there are 52 pieces in each Toobeez set)

Activity Instructions

1. Circle up the group, and share the following storyline with the group.

> You are a team of SCUBA divers in search of a chest full of gold lost by pirates over 300 years ago. When you come up to check on your salvage ship, you find that it has disappeared. Bad weather is moving in fast, and the waves are getting bigger. You will have to ride out the storm in the water until a rescue ship can arrive. You must gather your team as quickly as possible and get connected so that all team members are safe.

147

Bonus: Join Together

2. Read aloud the following Activity Challenge Box to the group.

> **Challenge**: The entire group must connect. Follow the guidelines below:
>
> - Participants must stay in physical contact with their piece of Toobeez throughout the activity
> - The group can not have any "satellites" that are not connected. Everyone must be connected in some way (like tree branches)
> - If any guidelines are broken, the group must begin again

3. To begin the activity, have participants first work through the Problem-Solving Sequence (refer to page 152 for the six sequence steps).
4. Have each person stand holding their piece of Toobeez to begin the activity.
5. If participants get stuck, have the students circle up again. Use questions to help guide the group back on track, but do not provide the participants with answers. Allow them to work together.
6. If your group is still struggling OR if you feel your group would benefit from an additional challenge, present the variation provided on the next page.
7. After the activity, move to the "Activity Discussion and Processing" section of the activity.

Bonus: Join Together

Activity Variations

1. Close your eyes.
After you give the group the basic activity (as described in the original activity), have them complete the challenge with their eyes closed.

Activity Notes

Acknowledgments
I developed this activity while working with a YMCA group.

www.project-connect.net   www.TeachMeTeamwork.com

Activity Discussion and Processing

Discussion Topic: Connecting with others

In the storyline, the participants must all "connect" in order to survive. In his 1999 book entitled *Connect*, Dr. Edward Hallowell, a psychiatrist and senior lecturer at the Harvard School of Medicine, provides a compelling case for the value of connections. Hallowell describes the research, which points to the great joy and peace that come from connecting and the consequences of remaining detached. He goes on to outline the steps we can take to make or reaffirm the connections that nourish our lives.

Discussion Questions

- What are the benefits of being or feeling "connected" (to family, friends, places, animals/pets, nature, ideas, etc.)?
- Do you know someone who lives a "disconnected" life? What is life like for them?
- On a scale of 1-10 (where 1 is no connection and 10 is the best connection possible), how would you rate your level of connection (your FEELING of connection) to your team? What would you like it to be? What is something you could do now to improve your feeling of connection to the team?
- What can the group do now to improve how strongly people feel connected to the team?

Motivator

In the activity, the group must connect in order to save everyone. Making connections and tending to them is one of the most important things we can do in our lives. If we look to nature, we see how everything is connected to each other. Contemplate the following quote.

- What is the importance of connection on your team and in your life?

"In nature we never see anything isolated, but everything in **connection** with something else which is before it, beside it, under it and over it." - *Johann Wolfgang von Goethe (1749-1832), German playwright, poet, novelist and dramatist*

150

Appendix

Supplemental Materials

Appendix A

Problem-Solving Sequence

Before the participants attempt an activity challenge, have the group work through the following six steps:

1. Circle up

2. Know and understand the challenge and the guidelines

3. Brainstorm

4. Make a plan

5. Do the plan

6. Evaluate results and adjust as necessary

Appendix B

Debriefing the Activity

One of the most important skills that an adventure facilitator can offer a group is the ability to help the group learn from and through the activity. This is often done through a "debriefing" process.

The debriefing process helps the group gain greater self-awareness AND move through the stages of development:

Form → Storm → Norm → Perform
(see page 167)

The goal of debriefing is to empower the group. Empowering means helping teams develop their skills and knowledge and supporting them to use their talents. Empowerment involves gradually turning over the responsibility for direction and support from the facilitator to the group.

You will NEVER have an empowered, self-directed group unless you are willing to SHARE control. *Empowerment is all about letting go so that others can get going.* Letting go may cause you to face the fear of *losing control,* which is a prominent fear for many traditional classroom educators.

Debriefing is an art, not a science, and it is often the difference between a good experiential learning activity and a great one. Here are some tips to help you create an optimal debriefing and processing experience:

1. **Prepare** - Prior to the group showing up, make sure you have all your materials together and you understand the activities you will be leading. This will reduce your stress level and allow you to focus on the interactions between people (rather than on the activity). Plan ample time for both the activity and the debriefing/processing.

2. **Circle Up** - Start and end the activity with the group in a circle. Make it a quality circle where everyone has a "front row seat." Have everyone

153

(even the facilitator) on the same level. If the kids are sitting on the floor, then the teacher should sit on the floor.

3. **Objective** - State the objective of the training/workshop/activity clearly. Make sure everyone understands what is going on and why.

4. **Names** - Make sure everyone knows each other's name. Wear name tags if you have to, and address people by their name.

5. **Timing** - Plan to process immediately after a major activity, however choose the best time to debrief and process the experience. If people are hungry and tired, you may need to take a break and re-visit the discussions. Vary the length of the debriefing sessions. Do not make a marathon out of each session.

6. **Environment** – Create an environment where participants are willing to share ideas and feelings.

   a. **Ground Rules** – Establish ground rules (what is said here stays here).

   b. **Tone of Voice** – Use a tone of voice that is welcoming and non-judgmental.

   c. **Encourage** – The leader sets the tone by encouraging everyone in a sincere way. All participants need to practice encouraging each other.

   d. **Respect Limits** – No coercion. Participants must be told that they can participate at the level at which they are the most comfortable. It is the facilitator's job to make the activity so compelling that everyone will want to participate.

7. **Share "Airtime"** – Most groups have difficulty making sure everyone has a chance to talk, be heard and be understood. To help your group learn how to share the available "airtime," teach them how to use a "talking stick." When someone has possession of the talking stick, they are the only one permitted to talk and everyone else must listen. When they are done talking, the stick is passed on to someone else who wants to talk. (You do not have to use a stick. I like to use a Koosh® ball because it is easy to toss and catch. You can use a Toobeez pipe section or a Toobeez ball, but do not allow people to toss these.)

8. **Listen Actively** – Many people are not really listening when someone else is talking. What they are really doing is waiting to speak. The leader must model how to listen actively. An active listener is able to repeat back what they heard (not like a parrot, but in their own words). The goal of active listening is to really understand what the other person is saying.

9. **Ask Questions** – Someone new to leading teambuilding games will usually tell the group lots of things about what they saw the group doing. An advanced

facilitator tends to ask powerful and insightful questions. They ask "open-ended" questions that require higher-level thinking. An example of an open-ended question is, "Which is heavier... 1,000 pounds or a heavy heart?" Ask your group open-ended questions that will get them thinking in new and creative ways. Get comfortable with the quiet period between your question and the time it takes for someone to respond.

10. **Feelings** – Learn to identify, acknowledge and honor your feelings and the feelings of the group members. In the world of advanced leadership development, this area of expertise is called "emotional intelligence." Extensive research shows that the most successful leaders have a well-developed emotional intelligence.

Why Did We Do That?

How to process teambuilding games

"Why did we do that?" It was the first question the group of 15 teenagers asked me after investing 90 minutes into completing the Spider's Web activity. My response? I bumbled around for a minute or so, mentioning buzz words like "teamwork" and "leadership," and I tried to explain how they would use this stuff once they returned home. They did not buy it, and I must confess, neither did I.

The year was 1987, and I was in my first year working for the Camp Woodson program in North Carolina, a wilderness-based, pre-release program serving adjudicated youth. Our job as camp counselors was to help the program participants learn and practice important life skills that would keep them out of jail and maybe even turn their lives around.

Like many new to the field of adventure learning, I found myself leading teambuilding activities that I had just learned (from a book or from other staff members). My greatest challenge was that I had very little knowledge about how to effectively help the participants learn from the activities. It was unclear to me how to "debrief" or "process" these activities with any degree of confidence.

Fortunately for me (and more importantly for the campers), my supervisor was present at that particular event to help bail me out. She skillfully led the group of teenagers through an amazing series of questions resulting in a dialogue that helped the students grasp the lessons they needed to learn. She was able to do this in a way that allowed the students to take ownership of the information, which I found magical. I decided then and there that I would learn to master group facilitation and that I would uncover the mystery behind the debriefing process.

Though I may not be at a stage of mastery, I have learned a few things about helping a group successfully navigate the debriefing process.

Appendix B

The following debriefing model is a direct result of my work with over 8,000 fifth-grade students in an in-school adventure-based learning program I developed and delivered for the YMCA of Western North Carolina between 1991 and 1996.

The program was called "Adventure Day," and the program's purpose was to help an entire class of fifth graders (about 25 kids) learn and practice specific strategies that would lead to greater team (classroom) harmony. The program utilized basic portable teambuilding activities (including the Hoop Pass, Pass the Can, All Aboard, Toxic Waste, etc.).

I would start the day off with a discussion about teams, asking the students to supply examples of "real-life" teams. The kids almost always mentioned sports teams as examples, and then the kids would start to give examples of people who work together in everyday life (doctors, policemen, firemen, construction workers, pilots, families, etc.). The purpose here was to set the stage for the key understanding that teams are everywhere in our society.

I would then share with the students that the Adventure Day program was really about a scientific journey to discover the specific <u>choices</u> in behavior that produce consistent beneficial results, both to the team and to each individual regardless of the activity challenge. This is when I would share with them the following "Results Diagram" which I would draw out on a giant piece of newsprint.

157

Results Diagram

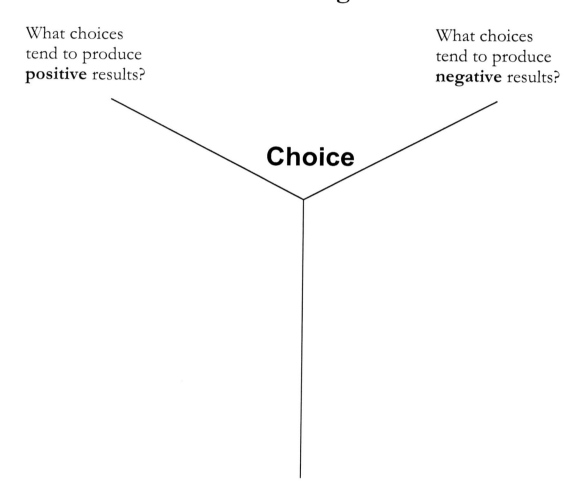

What choices
tend to produce
positive results?

What choices
tend to produce
negative results?

Choice

I would describe the diagram with the following analogy:
"If you were walking through the woods on a path (point to the vertical line in the diagram) and you came upon an intersection, you might decide to go right, left, backtrack or stand still. Today's program is all about moving forward (rather than standing still or backtracking), and it is about paying attention to what is happening as a result of your individual and collective choices. The Results Diagram will help us record the results of your choices for future reference."

www.project-connect.net   www.TeachMeTeamwork.com

I would return to the diagram throughout the day of teambuilding exercises both during and after nearly every activity. During these brief meetings, I would ask the students the following question, "What did you learn through this last activity that will help you on the next activity even though you do not know what the next activity is?" I was hoping students would recognize that their choices in behavior helped the team to succeed.

I stood with a maker in hand ready to record the student's thoughts on the newsprint. The students would initially come up with responses like "teamwork" or "communication," buzz words that they had been hearing for years from teachers and others. I always pressed them for specifics. "What specifically about teamwork?" I would inquire. Usually after a minute or two, their answers would include responses such as planning, sharing ideas and cheering each other on.

Sometimes, I would ask the question and a student would respond with an activity-specific strategy such as, "We need to hang on to each other and balance on the next activity." I would usually state that the next activity happens to have nothing to do with balancing and holding on to each other. This would require the student to come up with a suggestion that was applicable to any activity. For example, they might respond with answers such as helping each other, trusting each other, brainstorming together and so on.

As the day progressed, the activities became harder and more involved, and the group would often start to have difficulties. When difficulties arose, I would call a time out and have the group sit down to discuss what was going on. I would lead the discussion in a "charge neutral" (see page 161) fashion, always approaching the work from an inquisitive "scientific" standpoint. I would simply go back to the Results Diagram and ask, "What choices are you making now – either consciously or unconsciously – that are producing negative results?" Sometimes, the students would have to take a mental "step back" in order to answer the question. For some, it was a bit of a challenge to acknowledge that they were making choices that were hurting the team or causing some kind of negative result. Typically, the students would state that being mean, not sharing, being rude, not taking things seriously enough, and so on were affecting the team.

159

Appendix B

By the end of the day, the diagram was filled in with choices that produced positive results regardless of the circumstances and negative results. It was not uncommon for the classroom teacher to look at this and remark, "I tell them this stuff all the time!" The difference was now the students "owned" the information because they had generated it through their own teambuilding game experiences. They had vivid memories of which exercise produced a particular learning (piece of information).

The Adventure Day program was typically offered at the beginning of the school year, and the teacher usually posted the Results Diagram on the wall for reference throughout the school year.

The "Results Diagram" is simply a debriefing tool used to help the participants link behavior (choices) with specific outcomes (results). This task of helping kids develop a clear link between their choices and the outcomes was the drive behind the Adventure Day program. I have since come to believe that one of the most important services adventure programs can provide is helping participants see that success or non-success is a result of choices we are making, both on a conscious and unconscious level.

Since those days delivering the Adventure Day program, I have successfully used the Results Diagram with a wide range of groups – from fifth graders to corporate executives and everything in between. It seems that, regardless of the population, there are few who would not benefit from clarifying the link between their behavior (their choices) and the results of their behavior. The Results Diagram encourages people to "own" the fact that their choices have caused them to end up in the situations they experience on a daily basis.

The Results Diagram is based loosely on the work of William Glasser's *Reality Therapy*. The questions that Glasser developed for his therapeutic process were:
1) What do you want?
2) What are you doing to get what you want?
3) Is it working?
4) If it is not working, are you willing to try another approach?

160

Charge neutral vs. Charge up/down
- A concept developed by Coach University (www.coachu.com)

Charge neutral describes the tone of voice that has no edge or high or low energy to it. It is a useful communication style when coaching a student to make a huge change or to see something big. Charge neutral has an almost blasé feel, kind of like describing a boring weather day. "Oh, it is a nice today, is it not?" "Oh, your leadership style is a mess, is it not?" "Oh, we need to do a 180 here, do we not?"

One can be charge neutral and still be very passionate. One becomes charge neutral when they are comfortable with themselves, are not performing, have a strong personal foundation and so on. One can care a tremendous amount and still be charge neutral. Charge up (loud, reactionary, edge in voice, hyper, concerned, problem-oriented) and charge down (patronizing, parenting, diminishing, downing, passive) are what a person shifts from to become charge neutral. **Note:** When you are charge neutral, you can get away with anything (as in saying what needs to be said).

161

Appendix C

Introduction to Leading Adventure-Based Experiential Teambuilding Games

The Three Key Components of a Successful Teambuilding Activity

Fun

A great teambuilding activity is fun. It can still be fun if people are struggling, sweating and working hard. Fun means it engages the imagination.

Movement

Every great experiential teambuilding activity gets people moving and interacting with the space around them in a new or different way.

Risk/Challenge

A skillful leader is able to create a supportive and nurturing environment that encourages risk-taking, and there must be a degree of risk or challenge involved in the activity. This could mean falling backward into the arms of the group, or it could mean sharing a thought or feeling with the group. Set things up so people have opportunities to step outside their comfort zones.

Key Concepts of Experiential Learning

"Traditional" Model of Teaching

In more traditional models of teaching and leading, the teacher is seen as the definitive source of all pertinent information. The teacher passes knowledge on, and the participants learn it. The participants are usually passive and are generally viewed as receivers rather than learners.

Experiential Learning Model of Teaching

A holistic educational philosophy carefully chooses experiences supported by reflection, critical analysis and synthesis. The experiences are structured so the learner takes initiative, makes decisions and is accountable for the result. This is done through actively posing questions, investigating, experimenting, solving problems, assuming responsibility, being creative, constructing meaning and integrating previous knowledge.

The Learner

Learners are engaged intellectually, emotionally, socially, politically, spiritually and physically in an uncertain environment where the learner is free to experience success, "failure," adventure and risk taking. Learning usually involves interaction between learners, learner and educator, and learner and environment. The learner is challenged to explore issues of values, relationship, diversity, inclusion and community.

The Teacher

The primary difference between experiential learning and the traditional model of teaching is the teacher does not provide all the answers to the group. The participants learn primarily from each other and through the experience or activity. The teacher's primary roles include selecting suitable experiences, posing problems, setting boundaries, supporting learners, insuring physical and emotional safety, facilitating the learning process, guiding reflection and providing the necessary information.

The Primary Goal

The need for connection and love is the primary goal of all human beings. As a result, the primary goal of experiential learning is to help students connect at an even deeper level.

Dewey's Model of Experiential Learning

As you prepare to lead experiential teambuilding activities, it is critical to understand the importance of Dewey's Model of Experiential Learning (see diagram below). The sequence starts with the Concrete Experience.

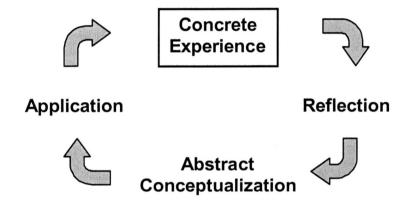

Concrete Experience	An action or interaction between the student and the environment, subject or teacher.
Reflection	The action is considered either through observation, reflection, debriefing (discussion) or some combination of these.
Abstract Conceptualization	Deriving some meaning or knowing from the experience, and integrating previously generated knowledge with the new experience.
Application	Testing the deductions made or applying what has been learned to new experiences.

Appendix C

Transformational Learning

I know you. You are an educator (teacher, trainer, facilitator, coach, etc.), and as an educator, you seek to help people learn. What is absolutely crucial, though, is <u>how</u> you help people learn. What type of learning environment are you creating for your students?

According to Don Wolfe, a famous change agent, there are only two kinds of learning:

1. Informational learning
2. Transformational learning

Informational learning is what you typically find in our education system. This is the type of learning I was trained to deliver while earning my teaching degree at a major university. The teacher talks and the students listen. Students take notes, take tests and are given grades. Informational learning focuses on the "head" (the brain).

Transformational learning is entirely different. By creating transformational learning experiences, the educator empowers students to discover answers for themselves. Transformational learning is slower and the results are much more profound. Transformational learning focuses on the "heart."

In their book, *The One Minute Millionaire*, Mark Victor Hansen and Robert Allen wrote about transformational learning...

> We live in the age of too much information and not enough transformation. When people get stuck, it's rarely because they don't know enough. It's because they lack the ability to act on what they already know. Transformational learning is not about taking notes in a notebook. It is about writing the lessons on your heart and in every cell of your body so that your behavior flows effortlessly, without compulsion, from the wellspring of your natural desire to live the life you were born to live.
>
> The main goal of transformational learning is to cause you to experience "ahas." An aha is when your awareness expands – when you "get it." The lights go on and you say to yourself, "Aha!"

To truly touch the lives of your students, you as an educator must create transformational learning experiences. The activities found in this guide are designed to help you create transformational (experiential) learning experiences.

Informational Learning *Traditional Classroom Education*	**Transformational Learning** *Experiential (Adventure) Education*
Left brain Intellectual Head Structured Serious Rigid Told the answer Repetition Passive involvement Hold back Fear Being *the* best Knowledge Uh-oh! Oh, no	Right brain Emotional Heart Creative Curious Spontaneous Discover the answer Intuition Active involvement Let go Trust Being *your* best Understanding Aha! Oh, yes

Source: *The One Minute Millionaire* by Hansen & Allen, © 2002

Appendix C

Stages of Group Development

Helping a team move through the stages of group development is one of your primary goals as a group leader (educator, teacher, trainer, facilitator, coach, etc.). There are four stages of group development. Each stage is unique and each stage requires different leadership skills.

The following chart identifies the four stages of group development along with tips for how the leader can help the team evolve.

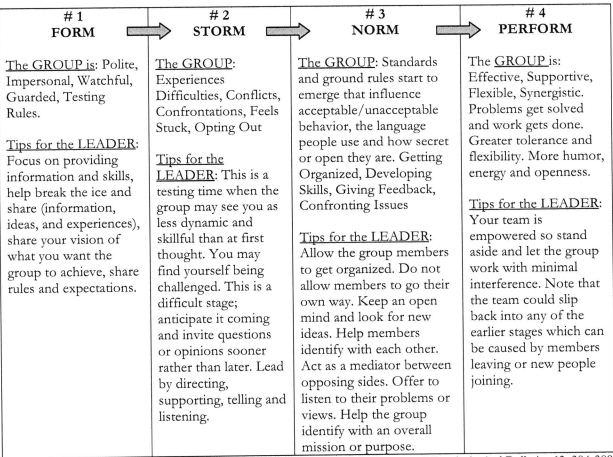

# 1 FORM	# 2 STORM	# 3 NORM	# 4 PERFORM
The GROUP is: Polite, Impersonal, Watchful, Guarded, Testing Rules. Tips for the LEADER: Focus on providing information and skills, help break the ice and share (information, ideas, and experiences), share your vision of what you want the group to achieve, share rules and expectations.	The GROUP: Experiences Difficulties, Conflicts, Confrontations, Feels Stuck, Opting Out Tips for the LEADER: This is a testing time when the group may see you as less dynamic and skillful than at first thought. You may find yourself being challenged. This is a difficult stage; anticipate it coming and invite questions or opinions sooner rather than later. Lead by directing, supporting, telling and listening.	The GROUP: Standards and ground rules start to emerge that influence acceptable/unacceptable behavior, the language people use and how secret or open they are. Getting Organized, Developing Skills, Giving Feedback, Confronting Issues Tips for the LEADER: Allow the group members to get organized. Do not allow members to go their own way. Keep an open mind and look for new ideas. Help members identify with each other. Act as a mediator between opposing sides. Offer to listen to their problems or views. Help the group identify with an overall mission or purpose.	The GROUP is: Effective, Supportive, Flexible, Synergistic. Problems get solved and work gets done. Greater tolerance and flexibility. More humor, energy and openness. Tips for the LEADER: Your team is empowered so stand aside and let the group work with minimal interference. Note that the team could slip back into any of the earlier stages which can be caused by members leaving or new people joining.

References: Tuckman, B. (1965). "Developmental Sequence in Small Groups." <u>Psychological Bulletin</u>, 63, 384-389. Blanchard, Carew, Parisi-Carew (1990). <u>The One-Minute Manager Builds High Performing Teams</u>.

Key Understandings of the Four Stages of Group Development

- The stages are predictable
- Each stage requires different skills from the group leader. If the group leader attempts to use the same style of leadership through the stages of group development, the group will evolve slower and it will be harder for the group members to become empowered
- No stage is better than any other. All are necessary and all are healthy
- The job of the group leader is to:
    - Help the group move through the stages of group development in a healthy (Class I*) way
    - Help team members develop skills and knowledge so they become self-directed
    - Provide/create an environment where team members feel willing to risk, grow, take responsibility and be creative
    - Empower team members by helping them develop their skills and knowledge and by supporting them to use their talents
- Groups can regress (for example, go from "performing" to "storming"). Causes include:
    - Group membership changes (someone is added or someone leaves)
    - Task changes
    - Major event occurs which disrupts group functioning
  When groups regress, the overall leadership style must change to match the needs of the group
- It is useful for groups to understand the Four Stages of Group Development model when the group is in the forming stage. When group members have this knowledge early on, the group is likely to evolve faster

* A "Class I" experience feels good, is good for you, is good for others and serves the greater good.

The Comfort Zone

While working for the YMCA in the mid 1990's, I had the opportunity to see many people join the Y with the intention of improving their health and wellness. Most had a desire to increase their strength and stamina and improve flexibility while losing weight.

These new members would take a fitness evaluation to help determine their current level of health. They were then encouraged to create a new goal for the level of health they now wanted to enjoy.

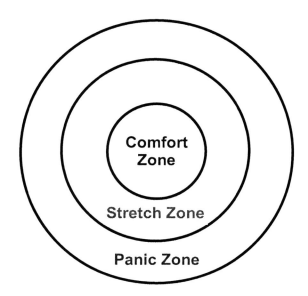

Occasionally, I would ask the most unfit and unhealthy people how they came to be so unfit and unhealthy. Many would respond with, "I allowed myself to get too comfortable" (or a variation on that theme). In nature, things are either growing or dying. There is no in-between. People (and teams) are the same way. Growth requires stretching, and stretching is not always comfortable.

When I work with a team, I share with them the above model, which graphically shows the Comfort Zone, Stretch Zone and Panic Zone. My job as a team coach is to provide opportunities for individuals and the team as a whole to step outside of their Comfort Zone and "play" in the Stretch Zone.

The Comfort Zone is a person's standard form of reference. This is the place where there is a complete absence of fear and anxiety. A person operating in the Comfort Zone feels 100% confident of their ability to perform a given task. There is a degree of boredom associated with this zone.

169

Appendix C

The team coach who leads adventure-learning activities should attempt to get the group to expand into the Stretch Zone because this is the zone where a majority of growth and learning happens. A skilled facilitator will present activities in a sequence that promotes a building effect, starting with "easier" activities and building to more "difficult" activities.

A great program design (and a great team coach) manages the energy of the group and guides them throughout the day in such a way that keeps the majority of people in the Stretch Zone as much as possible. To reduce the effects of negative anxiety, the participants must never be coerced or pressured into participation. Participation in an activity must always be by choice. Adventure leaders take people out of their standard form of reference (out of the "Comfort Zone") and ask them to engage in things that are new and different.

If the individual or group is asked to stretch *too* far, they will end up in the Panic Zone where little learning takes place due to overwhelming anxiety and fear. In the Panic Zone, the brain "down shifts" and higher-order thinking is not possible. Ideally, participants should spend no time in the Panic Zone. In the event that someone does end up in the Panic Zone, their recovery may be quick or prolonged. Oftentimes their trust in the program and the facilitator will be diminished.

To present this idea to a group, create three big circles on the ground and identify the circles as a Comfort Zone, Stretch Zone and Panic Zone. Then read out some events (see list below) and ask people to walk to the ring that represents how they would feel performing each event.

1. Handling venomous snakes
2. Swimming 100 yards across a lake
3. Talking to 100 people
4. Saying "I love you" to a total stranger
5. Relaxing at the beach
6. Singing in the shower
7. Cooking a meal for four
8. Solving word puzzles
9. Climbing a rock wall
10. Composing a song for a loved one

170

Appendix C

What you will find (and the group will discover) is that people respond differently to a given event. For example, if asked to give a presentation to 100 people, some will feel comfortable doing it while others will feel stretched doing it. It may even cause others to panic. If you present an event to the group that gets them to evenly distribute themselves, ask them to volunteer what it feels like to be in that zone. This sharing can help people to better understand the group members.

Finally, it is important to realize that these zones are not stagnant. More time invested in the Stretch Zone will result in either growth of the Comfort Zone (that is, what was once a stretch is now easy and comfortable) and/or growth of the Stretch Zone.

Appendix C

Eight Tips to Presenting an Experiential Learning Activity

1. Safety first! When participants do not feel physically and/or emotionally safe, learning is inhibited.
2. Create a learning environment free of coercion. One of the key ways to do this is to present the activity and allow people to participate at the level that is comfortable for them. Do not make participation a requirement.
3. Keep the rules simple and clear. Know when and how to change the rules.
4. Have lots of fun and people will learn in spite of themselves.
5. Stay flexible in your approach.
6. Present the activity, and then step back and allow the group to work (and sometimes stumble) through the challenge.
7. Allow enough time for the activity <u>and</u> the debriefing process.
8. Meet the group where they are and offer appropriate challenges. Most people in our culture have participated on teams that produce win-lose and/or lose-lose situations. The goal of adventure-based experiential learning is to produce sustainable and win-win thinking.

How NOT to Present an Experiential Teambuilding Activity

1. Provide too much information at the beginning of the activity so that participants have little left to discover for themselves.
2. Talk more than you listen.
3. Lead participants to the "classic solution" instead of allowing them to reach the goal in their own manner.
4. Process the experience in more detail than required.
5. Stop the activity frequently and tell the group what you think every five or ten minutes instead of waiting for the best teachable moment.
6. Encourage the group to be creative and then restrict their creativity with unnecessary rules or guidelines.

<u>Important Safety Information</u>

Visit <u>www.toobeez.com/safetyinfo.htm</u> for the latest safety information & product updates.

ATTENTION ALL USERS OF THIS PRODUCT:

- This product has been tested and approved for use with participants 4+ years of age
- Please inform all users of this product of this very important information
- Failure to obey or understand these legal disclaimers could result in bodily injuries
- This product was not designed to be a "climb-on" that you may see in a playground or schoolyard
- Using excessive weight or force on a structure could cause it to break and may void the warranty
- It is highly recommended that all structures be built on a flat and even surface at all times
- Do not use this product as a baseball bat, sword or any type of weapon. Please inform all users of this information
- Do not use this product to harm other people, animals or other personal property
- This product was not designed or manufactured as a "water toy" or as a water-safety flotation device. The tubes on this product will absorb water which will cause it to sink. Use of product in water is at your OWN RISK
- Please use this product in a safe manner to ensure years of fun

Product Information
This product is made of a high quality polypropylene and ABS thermoplastic material. This product also includes an ultra violet (UV) stabilizer to help minimize color fading due to excessive and direct sunlight. It is not recommended to leave this product in direct sunlight over long periods of time.

Product Care

Outdoor use: It is not recommended to leave this product in direct sunlight over long periods of time. Doing so will shorten the life of the product and possibly cause the plastic to become brittle, in turn causing the plastic to break. If this product is left in direct sunlight for extended periods of time, thermoplastics will absorb the heat. This product could become too hot to handle with bare hands. Please be cautious.

Storage: It is not recommended to store this product in a place where the temperature is not regulated, such as in a car on a hot day for an extended period of time. To avoid injury, try to avoid storing this product in places where heat can build up and be absorbed by the product.

Do not climb: Toobeez were intentionally designed as a "non-climbable" structure/building product. It is primarily used for building framework. That is why the ends on the tubes may come apart if you stand on the product or try to bend the ends forcefully into a sphere. This is a built-in safety feature and is not advertised (it is our patent-pending "company secret").

First-time Use

When using this product for the first time, it is highly recommended that an adult instruct all users how to properly assemble and disassemble a structure. Start building from the bottom up to complete your structure. When you are ready to disassemble a structure, you must always begin by removing pieces from the top and working your way down to the bottom. Please review the set up and take down instructions for more information.

As an educational tool, it is suggested that teachers, parents or guardians work with and teach the children who use this product how to build safe structures and other creative forms.

Assembly

It is very important that every time a tube is inserted into a sphere, the rotating end of the tube should be turned to secure (or semi-lock) the tube to the inside of the sphere. This is accomplished by turning the rotating end of the tube ¼ of the way around (or 90 degrees) in either direction. You should feel the "key" (located on the end of the tube) roll over the speed bumps located inside of the sphere. **Note:** This is not a 100% secure lock, and therefore this product is marketed as a "do not climb construction/structure product." If you do not feel the "key" roll over the speed bumps (located inside of the sphere), try using another "key hole" on the sphere until you have achieved success. If you still cannot feel the speed bump "semi lock" into the sphere, please do not use that particular piece. It may still be under warranty or have reached the end of its product lifecycle.

<u>Never attempt to remove the screws from the sphere(s)</u>, or the rotating ends from the tubes. This will permanently damage the product and will void the warranty. The ends of the tubes are to be used only at certain angles when in use with the spheres. If you try to force the tubes into a bad angle, this puts unwarranted stress on the sphere and on the tube ends and can cause one of the following actions:

- Pressure on the screws to become loose on the sphere (Screws can be re-tightened with a #10 Torx screwdriver (previous models) or by using a Phillips or flathead screwdriver. Be careful not to over-tighten the screws)
- Pressure on the "T," located on the rotating tube ends, may become bent or damaged if excessive weight and pressure is applied. If this occurs when you are attempting to lock a tube into a sphere, you may not feel the "T" rollover the bumps inside of the sphere
- The rotating ends may become separated from the tube. To fix, simply re-insert it into the tube and be careful not to pinch your hand

If any of these actions occur, we will conclude the product was "possibly" being used in an inconsistent manner for which it was designed or manufactured.

Would you like to share your Toobeez teambuilding game?

Send me your best description of your teambuilding game. If I select it for inclusion in the next volume, I will attribute the game to you.

Please send your ideas and suggestions for Toobeez teambuilding games to:

Tom Heck
tom@teachmeteamwork.com

We encourage you to contact the Toobeez™ Project Connect Joint Venture members for more product information or additional services. Additional contact information is available on pages 4-5 of this guide.

Tom Heck
Team and Leadership Coach and author of *The Official Toobeez Teambuilding Games and Activity Guide*. Tom trains educators how to lead engaging teambuilding games.
www.TeachMeTeamwork.com

Joseph A. Donahue
Project Connect Joint Venture Manager and inventor of the Toobeez™ giant construction building system. www.project-connect.net

Victoria Anderson, M.Ed.
Author of the *Toobeez Language Arts Activity Workbook* and consultant for Anderson Editorial Services, providing professional writing, editing and formatting services.
www.andersoneditorialservices.com

B. Michael McCarver, JD and Albert J. Reyes, MA
President and Chief Science Officer (respectively). Lingua Medica, LLC provides educational writing, research and analysis. Co-authors of the *Toobeez Math Activity Workbook*.
www.linguamedica.net

Timothy G. Arem, M.Ed., YFT
T-Bone Productions International provides health and fitness consulting and marketing services to schools, family fitness events and companies.
Author of the *Toobeez Physical Education Activity Workbook*.
www.TboneRun.com

Candice Donnelly-Knox, OTR/L
Candice is an occupational therapist serving the pediatric population in a variety of educational settings, combining fun and function to encourage independence.
Author of the *Toobeez Occupational Therapy Activity Workbook*.
Brainwaves4kids@aol.com

Vicky Pitner, CTRS
Recreation Services provides therapeutic recreation consulting, workshops, program development and more! Author of the *Toobeez Senior Therapy Activity Workbook*.
www.recreationservices.net

177